KU-411-159

Education, Persons and Society:
A Philosophical Enquiry

Glenn Langford

MACMILLAN

© Glenn Langford 1985

All rights reserved. No reproduction, copy or transmission
of this publication may be made without written permission.

No paragraph of this publication may be reproduced, copied
or transmitted save with written permission or in accordance
with the provisions of the Copyright Act 1956 (as amended).

Any person who does any unauthorised act in relation to this
publication may be liable to criminal prosecution and
civil claims for damages.

First published 1985

Published by
Higher and Further Education Division
MACMILLAN PUBLISHERS LTD
Houndmills, Basingstoke, Hampshire RG21 2XS
and London
Companies and representatives
throughout the world

Printed in Hong Kong

British Library Cataloguing in Publication Data
Langford, Glen
Education, persons and society: a philosophical
enquiry—(Modern introductions to philosophy)
1. Education—Philosophy
I. Title   II. Series
370'.1   LB880.L/

ISBN 0–333–34326–3
ISBN 0–333–34327–1 Pbk

CONTENTS

ACKNOWLEDGEMENTS

I am grateful to Signadou College, Canberra, for an invitation to deliver a short series of lectures there in September 1979; ideas developed for those lectures formed the basis of this book. I am especially grateful to Peter Isaacs, my host on that occasion, for his hospitality, support and encouragement. I would also like to thank Professor Ronald Atkinson and Glyn Bartlett for reading and commenting on a final draft of the book, Brian Carr and Mike Golby for very helpful discussion on various topics and the editor of the series, Professor D. J. O'Connor, for his patience, help and encouragement. Finally I would like to thank Mrs Peggy Martin for typing the manuscript.

The author and publishers wish to thank the following who have kindly given permission for the use of copyright material: Associated Book Publishers (U.K.) Ltd for an extract from *Gormenghast* by Mervyn Peake, published by Eyre and Spottiswoode; Faber & Faber Ltd for extracts from *Rosencrantz and Guildenstern are Dead* (1967) by Tom Stoppard; Pan Books Ltd for an extract from *The Hitch Hiker's Guide to the Galaxy* by Douglas Adams.

PREFACE

There are many different ways in which a book on philosophy of education might be written, emphasising different aspects of what is at best an ill-defined subject. Here I have taken as my basic theme the view that education is best thought of as a social activity or practice, the overall purpose of which is that of helping others to become persons. As the title of both the book and the final chapter suggest I have tried throughout to explore in different ways the connection between education, persons and society. In developing that theme, I have introduced a contrast in Chapter 2 between what I have called the Lockean and the Gombrich views. The Lockean view is put forward as a reasonable extrapolation of what I take to be Locke's basic position in the *Essay Concerning Human Understanding*, rather than as a faithful exegesis of Locke's expressed views on all of the questions discussed, in the belief that it is the former, or something like it, which provides the philosophical foundations of much recent work in the philosophy of education. What I have described as the Gombrich view is similarly based on remarks made by Sir Ernest Gombrich in *Art and Illusion* but goes beyond anything which he actually says. Although therefore I hope that he will not object to the way in which those remarks have been developed, I would like to make it clear that I cannot claim to be offering an accurate account of his actual views. I remain, of course, indebted to him for the use which I have made of his ideas.

CHAPTER 1   INTRODUCTION

'Many many millions of years ago,' according to *The Hitch Hiker's Guide to the Galaxy*, 'a race of hyperintelligent pan-dimensional beings . . . got so fed up with the constant bickering about the meaning of life . . . that they decided to sit down and solve the problem once and for all. And to this end they built themselves a stupendous super computer.' When it was finally completed the two chosen programmers, Lunkwill and Fook, approached it.

'"O Deep Thought Computer," Fook asked, "the task we have designed you to perform is this. We want you to tell us . . ." he paused, ". . . the Answer!"

"The Answer?" said Deep Thought. "The Answer to what?"

"Life!" urged Fook.

"The Universe!" said Lunkwill.

"Everything!" they said in chorus.

Deep Thought paused for a moment's reflection.

"Tricky," he said finally.'[1]

Although 'Life, the Universe and Everything' is not a bad description of what philosophy is all about, my concern here is more limited. The Universe and Everything (or at any rate most of it) lies outside its scope. However, I am concerned with at least some aspects of Life – with the lives people live, the social settings in which they live them, and the part which education plays in them. Indeed my immediate concern is with education and how best to conceptualise it; it is, in short, with the philosophy of education.

In Chapter 2 I try to lay down appropriate philosophical foundations for philosophy of education before going on in later chapters to look in more detail at particular aspects of education itself. During the last thirty years or so philosophy of education has been a very active, if still peripheral, branch of philosophy. Charles D. Hardie's *Truth and Fallacy in Education Theory*, first published in 1942 and republished in America in 1962, is generally accepted as a landmark in this respect. It was followed in this country in 1957 by D. J. O'Connor's *An Introduction to the Philosophy of Education* and in America in 1962 by Israel Scheffler's *The Language of Education*. Although of course there are differences, Hardie, O'Connor and Scheffler all share, very broadly, the same philosophical outlook, an outlook which I try to explore in Chapter 2 and refer to as the Lockean point of view. In doing so I make no attempt to do full justice to the complexity of Locke's own position; nor do I wish to suggest that the philosophers mentioned above are uncritical Lockeans. Indeed their immediate inspiration was almost certainly the logical positivism of the 1930s, epitomised in A. J. Ayer's *Language, Truth and Logic*. They do, however, share a commitment to the method of analysis and, more importantly, the atomistic metaphysic[2] which provides its justification and which, in turn, seems to be justified by the success of modern science. The result is an approach to philosophy of education which is highly individualistic in its outlook and which is unwilling to accept social phenomena as significant in their own right.

A second landmark in recent philosophy of education was the appointment of Richard Peters to the chair of philosophy of education at the London Institute of Education in 1962. His approach to philosophy is more eclectic and defies easy classification. Nevertheless it is true to say that he sees 'conceptual clarification' as 'pre-eminently the task of a philosopher of education' and that his own philosophy of education centres around his highly influential account of the concept of education, other ideas, such as that of teaching, being discussed in the framework thus provided. In that account he makes 'three conceptual points about "education" which [are] necessary for the explication of its essence.' They are that education 'relates to some sorts of processes in which a desirable state of mind develops'; that to be educated 'implies caring about what is worth while and being brought to care about it in a way that involves at least a minimum of understanding and voluntariness'; and that what is acquired through education should have 'a wide-ranging cognitive content'.[3] Even without examining this account in detail, two things about it are clear. First, it is concerned almost exclusively with the difference which being educated makes to an individual; and secondly, education is thought of as something which can be examined and described or analysed in isolation from any actual educational practice. Education is not therefore thought of as a social phenomenon and the idea of education is connected only with that of a person, or rather a person's mind, and not with that of society.

I have referred to the work of the philosophers mentioned above only in order to suggest that what is described in Chapter 2 as the Lockean point of view, or something like it, has provided the philosophical background to most of the philosophy of education of the last thirty years. Of course this is a crude generalisation which would need to be substantiated in detail before it could expect to be taken very seriously. My main purpose in describing the Lockean point of view, however, is to provide contrast with what I regard as a more appropriate alternative. That alternative, which I refer to as the Gombrich point of view, is intended to underpin the general approach to philosophy of education adopted in the chapters which follow. Gombrich is primarily an art critic and historian rather than a philosopher but I have used his name to describe the point of view which I try to develop because some of his remarks in *Art and Illusion*, quoted in the next chapter, point very clearly in that direction. Gombrich points out that we cannot understand the history of art – why, indeed, art *has* a history – without recognising the fact that painters paint as they do primarily because they have learnt to do so from their predecessors. In other words, painting is a social practice carried on in accordance with a social tradition; it is not the work of Lockean individualists guided only by their own personal vision and relying only on their own personal experience.

What is true of painting is true of other things, including, most relevantly, teaching. Teaching also, I suggest, must be thought of as a social practice carried on in accordance with a social tradition, and not simply as a transaction between otherwise isolated individuals. In other words, relations between teacher and teacher are as important for an understanding of education as relations between teachers and those they teach. It follows, if this approach is adopted, that it is the idea of teaching which must be taken as the starting point in philosophy of education, not that of education itself. Reference to education becomes necessary only in considering how teaching differs from other social practices such as medicine and nursing, social work and so on. It follows also that teaching is not wholly unique and that much can be learnt by comparing it with other social practices, especially those which, like teaching itself, are directed towards other people. Indeed the present study of teaching might be regarded as a case-study which might also be of use in trying to understand such practices.

The plausibility of the suggestion that teaching be taken as the starting point for philosophy of education clearly depends on the view taken of teaching. I would like therefore to introduce two models of teaching, suggested by the Lockean and the Gombrich approaches respectively. I will call the first the vertical or teacher-pupil model. According to this model, teaching is thought of as a face-to-face relation between a teacher on the one hand and a pupil or group of pupils on the other; the problem of giving a philosophical account of teaching is that of characterising that relation. Briefly, to teach is to help others to learn and, typically, to do so through the direct face-to-face interactions which take place in the teaching situation.[4] The Gombrich approach, however, suggests the possibility of a model of teaching which draws attention to the importance of relations between teacher and teacher and which will accordingly be called the horizontal or teacher-teacher model. As anticipated above, it suggests that teaching must be thought of as a social practice carried on in accordance with a social tradition. The problem then becomes that of giving a philosophical account of that practice. Briefly, a social practice is guided by a way of seeing and doing provided by a tradition; and teaching is distinguished from other social practices, for example medicine, by its concern for education rather than health.

Of the two models, it is the teacher-pupil model which seems obviously correct and which is taken for granted in most philosophical and psychological discussions of teaching. Indeed it is correct as far as it goes, provided it is complemented by the teacher-teacher model. If that is not done, and it is taken to represent the whole story, it is incomplete and becomes seriously misleading because it fails to recognise the importance of the more broadly defined context within which teaching encounters take place. The result is that the real meaning or purpose behind such encounters, which depends on their connection with education, is in danger of being ignored in favour of a narrow concern with technicalities. However, if the teacher-pupil model is incomplete unless complemented by the teacher-teacher model the reverse is also true. Any account of the practice of teaching which did not include a reference to the meeting between teachers and pupils which lies at its heart would also be incomplete, and without such a reference would not be recognisable *as* an account of teaching. Both models are inadequate on their own but each draws attention to what the other neglects.

To sum up, the philosophy of education is that part of philosophy which is concerned with our thinking about education rather than directly with education itself. The strategy to be adopted in the chapters which follow takes the idea of teaching rather than that of education as of central concern, but it will be successful only if teaching in turn is thought of as a social practice carried on by teachers in accordance with a social tradition rather than simply as an isolated transaction between individuals. This choice of strategy is based on philosophical considerations, not simply on convenience. The strategy rejected, that of taking the concept of education as central, and the vertical or teacher-pupil model of teaching associated with it, seems appropriate if an empiricist (or, as it will be called, a Lockean) position is adopted or taken for granted. In the next chapter an attempt will be made to set out the philosophical position on which the choice of strategy followed here is based and to compare it with the empiricist position normally taken for granted. Chapter 3 begins by distinguishing between philosophy of education, of which the present work is an example and which is a branch of philosophy, and *a* philosophy of education, which sets out to describe or modify a particular educational tradition. Two ways in which a teaching practice might be organised, either bureaucratically or as a profession, are then considered, while the final section of Chapter 3 considers the scope for technology in teaching and the need for a

curriculum. Chapter 4 considers the notion of accountability
and draws attention to its dependence on the idea of responsibility on the one hand and its connection with that of trust on
the other. Chapter 5 tries to delineate the notion of a role,
stressing the objective nature of roles and distinguishing between roles and their occupants. The first two sections of
Chapter 6 are concerned with the teacher-pupil model of
teaching, the third deals with learning, while the last draws
attention to the social nature of knowledge. A final chapter puts
forward a view about the overall purpose of a teaching practice,
the education of the young, and draws attention to the
connection between the concepts of education, persons and
society. Finally, at different places throughout the book an
attempt is made to develop an account of what I take to be the
central topic of philosophy of education, the concept of a person.

CHAPTER 2   PHILOSOPHICAL
FOUNDATIONS

I. THE GOMBRICH VIEW

The fact that the teacher is located within a tradition, and the extent to which teaching practice is governed by tradition, can be brought out by a comparison with the visual artist. In *Art and Illusion* E. H. Gombrich is concerned with what he calls 'The riddle of style', or the fact that 'not everything is possible in every period'. The art historian, he says, 'is concerned with the differences in style between one school of art and another', differences which it is his business to classify and describe. And he goes on to point out that 'we all react, to a major or minor extent, as he does . . . we see a Chinese landscape here and a Dutch landscape there, a Greek head and a seventeenth-century portrait'. This is so familiar a fact that it hardly seems worth pointing out. But it is less obvious why it is so; why, as Gombrich puts it, 'it is so easy to tell whether a tree was painted by a Chinese or by a Dutch master'.[1]

The explanation which he gives is that limits are set to the scope for innovation on the part of even the greatest painters by the tradition to which they belong. As he puts it, 'if art were only, or mainly, an expression of personal vision, there could be no history of art. We could have no reason to assume, as we do, that there must be a family likeness between pictures of trees produced in proximity' (Gombrich, pp. 3–4). And later he adds: 'The "temperament" or "personality" of the artist, his selective preferences, may be one of the reasons for the transformation which the motif undergoes under the artist's hands, but there must be others – everything, in fact, which we bundle together into the word "style", the style of the period and the style of the artist' (Gombrich, p. 55). Since the word 'style' might be thought appropriate only in the context of the visual and other arts, I will use the term 'tradition' to refer, more generally, to any settled manner of doing things.

What a tradition gives to a painter, in addition to and even more important than skills and techniques, is a way of seeing the world. He cannot avoid tradition, and the way of seeing that it lays down, simply by painting what is there. Gombrich quotes Constable himself as saying: 'The art of seeing is a thing almost as much to be acquired as the art of reading the Egyptian hieroglyphs' (Gombrich, p. 12). Later he remarks: 'All art originates in the human mind, in our reactions to the world rather than in the visible world itself, and it is precisely because all art is "conceptual" that all representations are recognisable by their style' (Gombrich, p. 76). Thus all seeing is seeing according to a certain way of seeing; ways of seeing must be acquired, as the Constable quote makes clear; and finally, perhaps only implicit in the above quotations but very important, ways of seeing must be acquired from and are therefore shared with others. It is these facts which explain why all pictures are painted in a recognisable style.

To acquire such a style, or to copy an archaic, existing style, is relatively easy. To introduce a new style – in other words a new way of seeing – is not, and it is the work of those who have managed to do so which provides the landmarks in the history of art. I have suggested that a way of seeing the world is given by tradition, but since traditions change it must be possible to see the world in different ways: as Gombrich says, the creative artist 'is the man who has learnt to look critically, to probe his perceptions by trying alternative interpretations both in play and in earnest' (Gombrich, p. 265). In illustration of this, he quotes an earlier art historian, Vasari:

> Taddeo always adopted Giotto's manner but he did not greatly improve it except in the colouring which he made fresher and more vivid. Giotto had paid so much attention to the improvement of other aspects and difficulties of his art that although he was adequate in colouring, he was no more than that. Hence Taddeo, who had seen and learnt what Giotto had made easy, had time to add something of his own by improving colouring. (Gombrich, p. 10)

Taddeo was able to make his own creative contribution, by 'improving colour', only because of the baseline provided by 'Giotto's manner of painting'. To emphasise tradition therefore is not to deny the possibility of creativity or change; rather they are made possible by tradition. Without tradition there would be nothing *to* change and no scope for creativity.

Of the two elements in a tradition or style of painting – skills and techniques, and ways of seeing – Gombrich emphasises the latter. Although I want to follow him in this, I do not want to deny that skills and techniques are important; innovative techniques, for example the introduction of new kinds of paint or different techniques for painting on wet plaster, are likely to go hand in hand with fresh ways of seeing. Obsession with technique, however, without any new vision, leads to sterility and stagnation. For the visual artist, a way of seeing the world is closely connected with his conception of his task as an artist – that of presenting the world as seen in that way in a manner which makes it available to others. Skills and techniques are primarily important because they allow him to do so more or less effectively, although mastery of them may be admired for its own sake. To be an original or creative artist is to see the world in a new way, rather than to be skilled in a technique, but a new vision may require the creation of fresh skills for its presentation in a work of art. The Sydney opera house, for example, was so new in its conception that it was unbuildable by the methods which then existed.

The main point which this consideration of Gombrich's views is intended to bring out is the importance of ways of seeing, or of conceptualising experience, even in the case of what is directly before our eyes, or before the eyes of a trained observer. We could, of course, speak equally well of language as structuring our experience, as Gombrich himself is tempted to talk about the language of art. To bring out the strength of the analogy between art and language he uses a drawing by Paul Steinberg 'in which a drawing hand draws a drawing hand which draws it. We have no clue as to which is meant to be the real hand and which the image; each interpretation is equally probable, but neither, as such, is consistent.' This is strikingly similar to the linguistic paradox of the liar, for example the statement written on a blackboard which reads: 'The only statement on this blackboard is untrue.' There is a limit to what a sentence can sensibly say about itself, which is exceeded here. Similarly, 'there is a limit to what pictures can represent without differentiating between what belongs to the picture and what belongs to the intended reality' (Gombrich, pp. 200–1).

Since language and visual representation are similar in this manner, what has been said about ways of seeing the world could be repeated for ways of describing it. Indeed, the two things are closely connected. As Edward Sapir put it:

Human beings do not live in the objective world alone, nor alone in the world of social activity as ordinarily understood, but are very much at the mercy of the particular language which has become the medium of expression for their society. . . . We see and hear and otherwise experience the world as we do because the language habits of our community predispose certain choices of interpretation. [2]

Frederick Waismann uses the following example to make the same point:

suppose there is a tribe whose members count 'one, two, three, a few, many'. Suppose a man of this tribe looking at a flock of birds said 'A few birds' whereas I should say 'Five birds' – is it the same fact for him as it is for me? If in such a case I pass to a language of a different structure, I can no longer describe the same fact. What, then, is the objective reality supposed to be described by language? [3]

It was pointed out earlier not only that all seeing is seeing in accordance with a way of seeing but that ways of seeing are acquired from and therefore come to be shared with others. The comparison with language brings this further point out very clearly. 'The language habits' to which Sapir refers are acquired when the young child learns the natural language of the community to which he belongs, and he can learn that language only through contact with others who are already competent in it. Language habits therefore are acquired from and shared with others, those others who belong to the same linguistic community. They are social habits, habits which are the shared property of a community, rather than the private property of individuals. Language habits, and the ways of seeing and experiencing the world which go with them, are shared with some, not all, other men. They are not the universal property of all mankind. In short, not all men share the same traditions.

Views similar to those outlined above have been expressed by many others. Here, however, I will refer to it as the Gombrich view.

II. THE LOCKEAN VIEW

I would now like to contrast the Gombrich view with what I will call the Lockean view, although I will offer only a simplified and perhaps simplistic version of Locke's own views. Locke, like Descartes, thought of a person as made up of a mind and a body. Both attached primary importance to the mind, although for Locke the body is also important since it provides access to the world outside the mind. The mind itself is defined in terms of its capacity for experience and is compared in turn with a sheet of white paper, a room and a mirror. Prior to experience the paper is unmarked ('void of all characters', as Locke puts it), the room is empty and the mirror reflects nothing. The mind comes to be furnished with ideas only through experience: that is, through the action of external objects on the body, especially the eye and other sense organs. This causes excitation first in the optic nerve and then in the brain, so producing 'in our minds the particular ideas we have of them' (that is, of external objects).[4] For example, light reflected from a dog on to the eye produces activity in the optic nerve and the brain and, eventually, the idea of a dog in the mind. All our ideas originate in experience in this way, either directly or indirectly.

Locke goes on to distinguish between different kinds of idea. In addition to simple ideas of sensation there are also complex ideas of reflection. Complex ideas are built up out of simple ideas or 'atoms of experience'. The mind can therefore acquire new ideas by its own activity but only in a mechanical way. Ideas of reflection are the result of the mind's awareness of its own activity (producing, for example, the idea of perception) and are thus a second kind of simple idea. The mind is also active in abstracting general ideas from ideas of particular things acquired through experience. General ideas are ideas of *kinds* of things which can therefore be applied generally to all things of that kind. For example, the idea of a cat is the idea of a kind of animal of which there are many instances. For present purposes general ideas may be equated with what we would now call concepts. So far as simple ideas are concerned, the mind is wholly passive; it acquires only those ideas which are presented to it by outer and inner experience and is incapable of inventing any new ones. Moreover, simple ideas, in being caused by the things they are ideas of, cannot fail to resemble them. All other ideas arise out of simple ideas. 'All those sublime thoughts which tower above the clouds, and reach as high as heaven itself, take their rise and footing here', that is, in simple ideas of sense and reflection.[5] Thus it is essentially correct to say that, for Locke, the mind is basically passive and incapable of invention. Its activity, in so far as it is active, is mechanical or pseudo-mechanical in nature.

One aspect of this account which deserves special mention is its atomism. The world *is* complex, as also is our experience of it; but this complexity is presented as the result of the combination of the simple elements which are the things which really exist. Locke tries to show how even our ideas of duration or time and of space are constructed out of simple ideas. Similarly, social groups and institutions, communities and their traditions, and so on are no more than the interaction of individuals whose own nature and existence does not depend on them. There is therefore a deep-rooted disinclination in the empiricist tradition which stems from Locke to take the social seriously, and this is clearly reflected in recent philosophy of education.

Locke introduces his account of language only after his account of thought is already complete. Men use words only to record their own ideas (and so to allow them to remember them more easily) and to communicate them to others. Words are 'sensible marks of ideas'; they stand for 'nothing but the ideas in the mind of him that uses them . . .', although men think they stand for 'ideas in the minds also of other men' and 'for the reality of things'.[6] Thus language is no more than the outward expression of thought which is already fully formed and which therefore owes nothing to it. The way we talk about the world reflects the way we think about the world; the way we think about the world depends on the way we experience the world; the way we experience the world depends on the way the world is. And the way the world is is wholly independent of any conventions or social traditions which we may have.

Thus Locke supposes that there is a one-to-one correlation between objects in external reality and simple ideas which they produce in the mind, and similarly between ideas in the mind and words. Given this view it would be very natural to suppose also that ideas resemble the things which cause them, just as the mark made by a signet ring resembles the signet ring itself.[7] Locke's attraction to this view is implicit in his analogy between the mind and a mirror, although in fact he held it only for so-called primary qualities. If this further move is made then, contrary to Gombrich's view, a painter *could* paint 'direct from nature', representing what was there directly and without alteration. Suppose, for example, he were painting a picture of a cat. The cat would produce an idea in his mind which would be a kind of mirror image of the cat; and he, in turn, would simply reverse the order of causality to produce an external representation of his idea of a cat. The net result would be that the picture of the cat would resemble the cat itself.

According to Locke, reality imposes itself directly on the mind of the individual, furnishing it with its basic materials, which it then arranges and rearranges according to mechanical or pseudo-mechanical principles. How things are seen depends solely on the individual's contact with reality; neither the painter nor anyone else needs to be supplied with a way of seeing by a social tradition. Art *could* therefore be 'only . . . an expression of personal vision' and there would be no such thing as the history of art. According to Gombrich, on the other hand, what we see depends, quite literally, on the way we have been taught to see. Seeing depends on a way of seeing which is aquired from others, and ways of seeing are the property not simply of individuals but of communities which have traditions and histories.

Gombrich is quite clearly correct in supposing that there is such a thing as the history of art and therefore has grounds for arguing that art cannot be 'only . . . an expression of personal vision'. His view gains further support from the evidence of ambiguous figures which can be seen in different ways, even although the pattern of stimulation on the retina of the eye remains the same. An example used by Wittgenstein in the *Philosophical Investigations* is that of the 'duck/rabbit' – a person looking at the same lines drawn on paper sees either a duck or a rabbit.[8] A second example is that of a two-dimensional representation of a three-dimensional object such as a cube. We see it as a cube but only because we are familiar with the conventions governing such representations – because we have learnt to see it that way. We can also see it as a flat six-sided figure with three lines drawn on it, although this takes a considerable effort of imagination. Gombrich himself quotes these and many other examples. A slightly different kind of example is provided by investigations into the visual memory of chess players conducted by Chase and Simon in 1973. Good chess players have better visual memory of board positions than bad players – but only of true board positions taken from actual games of chess. They have no special ability to remember random arrangements of the same individual pieces. What they are good at remembering, therefore, is not conceptualised visually but in purely chess terms such as attack, defence, control and so on.[9]

These examples suggest that there is no one way in which reality must be seen. What in one sense is the same thing, for example chess pieces on a board, can be seen either simply as a visual pattern or as a position in a game, depending on how we have learnt to see things. And we learn to see things as we do from others who already see them in that way.

III. LOCKE AND GOMBRICH COMPARED

The issue between Gombrich and Locke cannot be settled by drawing attention to the phenomenon of ambiguous figures. There is some truth in both positions if they are properly presented, although I have tried to emphasise the insights of the Gombrich view because I think that they are especially relevant to an understanding of the practice of teaching. I would like now to consider what might be thought a difficulty for that view and at the same time to show that on the question of whether the mind is active or passive in perception their views can to some extent be reconciled.

According to the Lockean view as I have outlined it, each individual builds up a picture of the world or a way of seeing things through his own personal experience. Strictly speaking, a person has access only to his own ideas; he does not have access to those of anyone else or to the causes of those ideas in the external world. There is no way in which he can compare his ideas with those of anyone else or with their causes. Strictly speaking, therefore, he has no reason to suppose that his picture of the world is the same as anyone else's, that it is accurate or, indeed, that there *is* an external world. This indeed is the conclusion drawn by Locke's successors, Berkeley and Hume. Locke himself, however, does not draw these conclusions, and it could be argued that he is right not to do so. Instead, his position is that of strict realism. Each person builds his own picture of the world, but there *is* a world of which it is a picture and it is the *same* world for everyone. Moreover, each person's picture of the world is constructed according to mechanical or pseudo-mechanical principles which are also the same for everybody. The result is that, allowing for individual differences in experience, one person's picture of the world is the same as anyone else's, and everyone's picture is objective in the sense that it was caused by and therefore accurately mirrors the same independently real world. The sense of objectivity concerned might be called the strong, or Lockean, sense. The way we see the world is determined directly or indirectly by the way the world is: by reality.

According to Gombrich, on the other hand, those painting at the same time see the world in a similar way because they learnt to do so from others who were already members of a social tradition. By the same token, however, those painting at *different* times see the world differently. Gombrich's view involves a kind of social relativism and so, it might be thought, leaves no room for objectivity. Acceptance of that view might even be thought to require acceptance also of the view that reality is a construction of the human mind. Therefore it is important to be clear about what relativism of the Gombrich kind involves. Firstly, it has been argued that a *way of seeing* reality, not that reality itself, is provided by a social tradition and in that sense is a social construction. A way of seeing can be made use of in actual seeing only in the appropriate circumstances; for example, a spider can be seen as a spider only when there is a spider to be seen in that way. Whereas there may well be a sense in which the way of seeing according to which a spider is seen as a spider is a social construction, it would be absurd to suggest that the spider itself is also a social construction. Secondly, ways of seeing have evolved rather than been constructed and were evolved in the first instance as part of man's long-term strategy for survival in a hostile world. The manner in which they evolved therefore was subject to severe external constraints and not all ways of seeing are equally viable: they have not evolved or been constructed arbitrarily. Thirdly, social relativism of the kind discussed does not mean that the *individual* can conceptualise reality in any way he pleases. Therefore it does not involve subjectivity. Each individual approaches reality with a way of seeing which, so far as he is concerned, is given. Since reality itself is also given it follows that his judgements, in so far as they are correct, are determined independently of his will, although there is scope for error, both wilful and inadvertent. Although it is true that we impose a structure on what we see rather than simply seeing what there is to be seen, it is also true that perception is passive. When we see, in so far as we see correctly, we see only what is there to be seen. Understood in this way, relativism is consistent with objectivity, although not, of course, with objectivity in the strong, or Lockean, sense distinguished earlier.

Although what we can see is determined by a way of seeing provided by a social tradition, what we actually see in making use of that way of seeing is determined by reality. The mind is active in making use of principles for organising experience but it is passive in being dependent on reality for its experience. The Lockean emphasis on the passivity of perception is not therefore wholly misplaced. Indeed, perception must be passive in this way if it is to be a source of knowledge. What we see must depend on what is there to be seen, not on ourselves, if it is to inform us as to the facts, but the facts only become available to us through a way of seeing which we must provide ourselves. We do not and cannot have any neutral access to them – that is, any access to them which does not depend on a way of seeing and which is therefore neutral as between different ways of seeing.

IV. WAYS OF SEEING AND WAYS OF DOING

There is a sense in which the Gombrich view is concerned with human activity in a way in which the Lockean view as so far outlined is not. Gombrich is concerned with painting. Painting, he says, is not, or not mainly, an expression of personal vision; it is carried on in accordance with what I have called a social practice from which the painter acquires not only skills and techniques but also a way of seeing. That is the only reason why Gombrich, as an art historian, is concerned with ways of seeing. But painting includes more than just seeing, whatever account is given of seeing. It also involves the representation of what is seen (what Gombrich calls the motif) in a picture, and this involves the painter in the use of tools and materials such as brushes, paint and canvas. It is for this reason that the painter needs skills and techniques as well as a way of seeing. It is because we associate the idea of painting so closely with the production of actual pictures that it is easy to overlook the importance of the ways of seeing to which Gombrich draws attention. It is only through paintings themselves, which are spatio-temporally located objects with an existence independent of their original producer, that others have access to the painter's vision. And the production of paintings is a practical activity in a way in which simple seeing is not.

There is a distinction to be made between seeing the world and being active in relation to it. As pointed out in the previous section, although seeing is active in making use of a way of seeing, it is passive in the sense that what is seen is determined by reality. Nor, in general, is what is seen changed in being seen. Constable, for example, saw Flatford Mill in a certain way but the mill itself was not changed because of this. What was changed was the canvas on which he worked when, making use of his skill as a painter, he transformed it into a picture of Flatford Mill. But whereas, given a way of seeing, what is seen depends on reality, what is done is not determined by reality in the same way. It is true that things can be changed only if they are there to be changed and that, barring miracles, they can be changed only within limits laid down by the kind of thing they are. Hence the saying, you can't make a silk purse out of a sow's ear. Within those limits, however, the way in which the canvas changed depended on the way in which Constable chose and, given his skill as a painter, was able to change it. In making his choice, however, he made further use of the way of seeing originally employed in seeing Flatford Mill itself. A way of seeing makes it possible not only to see things as they are but also to construct a vision of how they might be, a vision which in turn is changed into reality by the painter's activity.

Gombrich himself makes no explicit distinction between seeing and doing, at least so far as I can recall. This is presumably because, although denying that the artist can simply paint directly from nature, he is assuming that the way the artist sees nature, making use of a tradition of seeing, determines or largely determines how he paints it. Constable looked at Flatford Mill *as a painter* and therefore he saw it as a subject for a painting in a certain style; having done this all that remained was for him to use his skill to bring that painting into being. That is to say, he did not conceive of the techniques and skills at his disposal as neutral instruments, to be used without constraint in any way he chose. It is true that the same skills and techniques can be used in different ways. In the first book of the *Republic* Socrates points out that a doctor's medical knowledge and skill can be used not only to help others but also to harm them. 'Does not the ability to save from disease', he asks, 'imply the ability to produce it undetected?'[10] The answer is that if we ignore the practice of the medicine with which that ability is in fact connected then of course it does. But we do not expect it to be used in that way, since we think of a doctor as someone who is concerned to help others, not to harm them. Similarly, the doctor himself sees his patient not simply as suffering from a particular disease but also as a patient and therefore as someone to be helped. Within the context of the practice of medicine he cannot but see things in that way. Thus the way of seeing which a practice provides is not neutral so far as possible action is concerned. It is also a way of doing which guides and structures practice and therefore largely dictates the use to which the skills and techniques which it also provides are to be put.

The Lockean account, on the other hand, offers an account of seeing which in itself is totally divorced from behaviour. Lockean man as so far presented is motivated only, if at all, by disinterested curiosity. Such a picture is at best incomplete. It is as obvious to Locke as to anyone else that man does have practical concerns, but there is no reference to them in the original account of perception. An account of behaviour *can* be given, but if so it must be added to something already complete. The general lines which such an account must follow are clear. First, men must be credited with desires. External objects act on the body to produce not only ideas in the mind but also pleasure and pain, and in general, what men desire is pleasure and the avoidance of pain. The satisfaction of desire is the only end of action. Secondly, through experience knowledge can be gained not only of the perceptible properties of things in the external world but also of their power to cause pleasure or pain in us. Thirdly, in having the power of self-movement man can seek out those things which lead to pleasure and avoid those which lead to pain so that the amount of pleasure which is experienced is maximised and the amount of pain which is experienced is minimised. An immediate objection to this account is that men are said to desire only pleasure and the avoidance of pain, and this is almost certainly too narrow. But even if it is replaced by the view that men desire only what is in their own interests the basic position remains the same. In any situation in which he finds himself a man will decide what to do by consulting his own interests or desires, on the one hand, and the means available for their achievement, given his situation, on the other. He will engage in a 'cost-benefit' analysis, setting off expected costs (such as the pain of effort) against expected benefits from pursuing one course of action rather than another. Lockean man is a rational individualist, having the power of choice and deciding for himself what to do and how to do it, and doing so solely on the basis of his own nature and powers.

Therefore, according to Locke the relation between seeing and doing is very different from that suggested by Gombrich. What is seen depends only on what is there to be seen; it does not depend on a way of seeing and consequently is wholly neutral so far as any possible course of action is concerned. As a result whereas there is every reason to suppose that two people at the same place at the same time will see the world in the same way, there is less reason to suppose they will behave in the same way. They will do so only to the extent that their desires coincide. There is some reason to suppose that they will in fact do so, since all men share basically the same physiology. For example, both may be hungry and consequently will eat if there is food available; both may be afraid in the presence of a marauding tiger and may run away, and so on. They will behave differently, however, if one is hungry and the other is not, or if one wishes to prove his prowess as a hunter whereas the other does not, and so on. Thus in so far as men desire different things for themselves they will also behave differently.

Gombrich and Locke differ not only in their account of perception but also in their account of behaviour. In giving an account of a way of seeing, Gombrich is taking it for granted that a way of seeing the world brings with it a way of behaving in relation to the world; for example, the way Constable saw the world determined the way he painted. More generally a way of seeing is also a way of doing. Accordingly, everything which has been said about the connection between a way of seeing and a tradition or social practice applies also to doing. We not only see but also behave in the way we do because, first and foremost, that is the way people see and behave in the tradition to which we belong. Locke, on the other hand, gives a very different account of the relation between perception and behaviour. Behaviour may depend on perception (we need to see what we are doing) but perception does not similarly depend on behaviour. In this sense his account may be described as intellectualist. The way we see the world depends only on our own individual experience of it, leaving the question of how we are to behave in it to be decided on the basis of further, independent considerations. It is to be expected that the same objects will affect different people in roughly the same way not only in producing the same ideas but also in producing pleasure or pain and, since men also share the same, or roughly the same, powers of rationality, the result is that as a matter of fact we all tend to behave in roughly the same way. But there is no reason why we must do so. The painting of pictures, for example, would be 'only . . . an expression of personal vision' and there would be no reason to expect that anyone else, including those painting in the same period, would share the same vision.

V. THE INDIVIDUAL AND SOCIETY

1. Critical and conservative traditions

In drawing attention to the 'riddle of style', Gombrich reveals the inadequacy of any account of the history of art as the story of a succession of individuals guided only by their own personal vision. It might be objected, however, that in emphasising tradition in this way he leaves no room for individuality and consequently denies the importance of the creative artist. This is not the case. Clearly there could be no tradition – or history of art – if painters such as Giotto and Constable had not painted actual pictures on particular datable occasions. Even though in doing so they made use of a way of seeing and doing provided by the tradition to which they belonged, each picture was the result of a separate endeavour and each in varying degree reflected the painter's own personality and experience. As a result each picture, unlike a rug made from a traditional design, has its own character and detail. It is therefore possible for the way of seeing which a tradition provides to be modified not only by external influences – exposure to primitive or Chinese art, for example – but from within, through the personal vision and creative activity of its most outstanding practitioners. The history of art is in fact the history of such modifications. Creative in- dividuality of one sort or another is made possible by the relevant tradition rather than being ruled out by it.

To emphasise tradition is not in itself to deny individuality. As a matter of fact, however, it must be admitted that traditions differ greatly in the scope which they provide for individual expression. In what will later be called critical traditions such expression is permitted or even encouraged, whereas in what might be called conservative (or 'traditionalist') traditions it is discouraged or even forbidden. The painters who provide the landmarks in the history of European art are those who have contributed to and therefore changed the tradition to which they belonged. A rug made according to a traditional design, on

the other hand, will be made as it has always been made, so long
as that remains possible; the aim is to conserve the tradition
rather than to change it. The distinction between critical and
conservative traditions, however, does not affect the overall
position, although it is important in its own right. Acceptance of
the importance of tradition does not involve a denial of
individual action and effort. It means only that in trying to
understand what the individual does we have to see it as part of a
social practice governed by a tradition. The individual does
decide what to do and how to do it, but the opportunity of doing
so is provided by the tradition and in doing what he does he is
guided and constrained by the way of seeing and doing which
the tradition provides.

2. *Locke's account of social relations and social order*

Lockean man, on the other hand, has been presented so far as a
rational individualist who decides what to do only on the basis of
his own desires and the means available for their satisfaction.
But since it is obvious that men do interact with one another in
some way, the Lockean account must be extended to include
some account of social relations between men. Since the things
which men desire, such as food, shelter and sexual partners, are
likely to be in short supply, they will be forced to compete with
one another for them and may be expected to see each other as
rivals. But for a number of reasons the supply of some things can
be increased through co-operation. First, two people acting
together can sometimes do things that would be difficult or
impossible on their own, for example, using a large fishing net.
Secondly, as Plato pointed out in the *Republic*, people become
more efficient if they stick to one thing, such as fishing or
farming, relying on exchange for the other things which they
need.[11] Thirdly, exchange, in turn, depends on the mutual
recognition of the other's right to whatever is offered or received
in exchange. A further need – the need for the secure enjoyment
of property – which can only be met by some kind of co-
operation is generated in this way. It is this need, as Locke
suggests in his *Second Treatise of Civil Government*, which explains
why men consent to government and the laws which governments make, even although their freedom to act in their own
best interest is thereby reduced. They do so because the loss of

freedom is more than outweighed by the gain in security, for both persons and property, which results.[12]

The general picture which emerges is that men do enter into relations with one another but they do so only in order to achieve pre-existing desires more efficiently; in other words, in order to improve their situation while remaining unchanged in themselves. Thus although men do enter into social relations with one another, the sense in which such relations are social is minimal. There are such things as social groups and practices but they consist only of the individuals who are their members or practitioners and the ways in which such individuals happen to be related to one another. The view of the social thus follows the original account of the human mind, which comes to be furnished with complex ideas through the mechanical or quasi-mechanical combination of the ideas given in experience. According to the Lockean view any complex entity, whether an idea, a piece of behaviour, or a social group or practice, is to be understood only by breaking it down into its simple components which can then be understood in isolation. Men do have contact with other men but an understanding of that contact is to be gained by considering what they are in themselves as men; and that owes nothing to their relations with others.[13]

According to the Lockean account, the appearance of social order is simply the result of co-operation and competition between rational individualists, each acting as an individual but taking into account the presence of other such individuals. This view becomes more plausible in so far as it can be argued that there exists a mechanism which produces order out of the otherwise unco-ordinated behaviour of individuals. The best example of such a mechanism is the price mechanism which regulates supply and demand in the market place. In an ideal free market (one containing large numbers of buyers and sellers each acting independently but with complete knowledge of the situation) those who wish to buy or sell any commodity, whether goods or labour, can do so at a price determined impersonally by the relative strength of supply and demand. Every decision to buy or to sell is made by an individual acting independently of all other buyers and sellers and motivated only by his own interest. But the result is that supply and demand are equated at a single price which is the same for everybody. Order is thus

generated out of the unco-ordinated actions of rational individuals; the single price which rules in the market at any given
time is the unintended consequence of the intentional actions of
many separate individuals. The order concerned is clearly an
economic order and is generated out of the economic behaviour
of individuals (i.e. behaviour concerned directly with their own
material needs). It illustrates, however, the way in which the
Lockean account might be developed in the most favourable
case.

3. The need for practical principles

The market mechanism sketched briefly above operates to fix
not only the price of finished goods but also that of labour and,
indirectly, the level of the profits which are the rewards of
enterprise and management. The market therefore operates to
fix not only the level of prices but also the distribution of
incomes. The way in which incomes are distributed will depend
only on the operation of impersonal market forces; it does not
reflect a decision on anybody's part that it is *desirable* to
distribute incomes in that way. It is obvious, however, that
people may wish to criticise the distribution of income or other
aspects of the economic order which results, for example, as
being unfair or dehumanising. The Lockean account needs to be
further extended to take account of this possibility.

One way of doing this is by introducing the idea of a natural
harmony of interests, the result perhaps of the intervention of a
hidden hand. It might be claimed that, given such a natural
harmony, if each individual pursues his own interests then the
interests of every individual will be best served. The impersonal
mechanisms of the market operate automatically not only to
produce order but to do so in a way which is in the best possible
interest of all concerned. Everyone is justified, therefore, in
consulting only his own interests in deciding what to do, since
only if he does so will the interests of others be served best. The
early Lancashire mill-owners, for example, were justified in
paying low wages and employing child labour by the so-called
iron law of wages. If, moved by pity for the misery of the poor,
they increased wages they would become uncompetitive and go
out of business, with the result that their workers would lose

what little they had. Things always turn out for the best provided the hidden hand is allowed to act without interference. It follows that manufacturers should not pay their workers any more than they can help and the activity of government should be limited to the maintenance of law and order.

The idea of a hidden hand or natural harmony of interests is in many ways attractive from the Lockean point of view. The Lockean account is primarily an account of how the mind comes to be furnished with ideas – the ideas which form the raw materials of thought, belief and knowledge – through experience. Ideas are acquired through the action of external objects on the mind; they are impressed on the mind, like the design impressed on wax by a signet ring. The mind is therefore passive, untroubled by desire. But men are not wholly passive, they also have practical concerns and active powers which enable them to pursue those concerns, and they must therefore be credited with desires. They can then decide what to do on the basis of their desires, on the one hand, and, on the other, on their perception of their situation; having decided, they can then act accordingly. In short, self-interested desires are the only guide to conduct, and in so far as we deliberate about what to do, a reference to our desires plays a crucial part in our deliberations. However, as has been pointed out above, we may wish to criticise the social situation which results when everyone behaves in that way and this appears to suggest that there are considerations other than those of self-interest on which our conduct might be based. The natural harmony view is therefore attractive because it allows the Lockean to take this suggestion seriously without requiring any account to be given of such considerations. If any attempt to act on them is bound to be self-defeating, belief in such principles is misguided and there is no need to take them seriously.

Nevertheless the admission that conduct might be based on considerations other than self-interest – on principles of practice – is a substantial one from the Lockean point of view. This becomes obvious once it is realised that the laws of economics, although they cannot be ignored, do not control us as tightly as had been supposed. For example, since the rise of the unions it is now clear that there is scope for wage bargaining and that wage rates depend, at least in part, on relative bargaining strength. It would therefore have been possible for the mill-owners to have improved the lot of their workers had it not been for their belief in the rigidity of economic laws.

Moreover, reliance on market forces does not make equally good sense in all spheres. Whether or not the laws of economics make principles of practice irrelevant in the economic sphere, the need for them elsewhere remains. It was pointed out earlier that the exchange of goods in the market place depends on the mutual recognition, on the part of the parties engaged in it, of the other's right to whatever is offered or received in exchange. What changes hands in the market is the right to property, and it does so by voluntary agreement; in other words, theft and deception are ruled out. This being the case, someone who has been swindled, for example, must be able to claim redress. This need is recognised in courts of justice. But a court of justice cannot be thought of as just another market place. Of course officials can be bribed, just as property can be stolen, but that is a corruption of justice, not justice itself, just as stolen property does not become the property of the thief in the sense of giving him a right to it.

It is not surprising that all governments, even those most committed to the market mechanism, accept responsibility for the maintenance of law and order, but in doing so they cannot avoid a commitment to justice. There is a similarly strong case for arguing that national defence must be organised nationally and therefore that governments cannot avoid direct responsibility for external security. Other cases are less clear. Services as well as goods can be bought and sold, for example, medical, educational or even spiritual services. If they are, then the form which they take and how they are distributed will depend largely on who is willing (and able) to pay for what. But although medical and educational provision *can* be left to the free play of market forces, governments commonly accept responsibility, wholly or in part, for them, and accordingly finance their provision out of taxation. They then have to decide what to provide, and to whom, and need some basis on which to do this. It follows that some account of that basis must be given if the Lockean account is to make any claim to completeness.

VI. THE LOCKEAN ACCOUNT OF PRACTICAL PRINCIPLES

1. *Knowledge of practical principles*

The Lockean account of practical principles should in consistency follow the lines already laid down, according to which all ideas originate, either directly or indirectly, in experience. However, we can have experience only of those things which are available to be experienced. For example, for it to be possible for us to have the experience of seeing a cat there must be a cat for us to see. The cat must belong to the 'reality of things', to use Locke's phrase; it must be part of the independently existing world which we find out about through experience. If what is true of cats is also true of practical principles, they too must belong to the reality of things. They cannot, however, belong to it in the same way; unlike cats, they are clearly not available to act as objects of sense experience. Some other, non-sensory faculty must be introduced – a faculty of moral sense or reason perhaps – which will allow us to find out what the world, although in this case the world of values rather than the physical world, is like. Then the new extended picture of the world which results will be objective in the same strong, Lockean sense as the original picture of the physical world. Since practical principles are to be discovered by moral sense or reason rather than through the ordinary senses they may be described as *a priori* principles.

This account is attractive in that it presents values and the practical principles which express them as objective; there really is a right and wrong about what should be done which can be discovered by reason. It is not, however, free from difficulties. It involves the introduction of a whole new world, a world of values, in addition to the ordinary world of physical things, and whereas common sense requires us to believe in the latter it hardly requires us to believe in the former. It also requires the introduction of a new faculty, of moral sense or reason, to allow us to find out about that world, although without its being made clear *how* it allows us to do so. In the case of senses such as seeing and hearing it is possible to point to a corresponding organ of sense and explain how it works but no similar account is possible in the case of moral sense or reason. Indeed a different and, within its limits, more acceptable means-end view of reason was implicit in the account of behaviour already given. We use reason to decide what to do (what means to employ) in order to get what we want (to achieve the ends set for us by our desires); to reason is to deliberate about the means to be adopted to achieve given ends. So there is no reason, apart from the need to find out about the world of values, to suppose that there is any such thing as a faculty of moral sense or reason. Moreover if there were such a faculty which was common to all men, we would expect that all men would assent to the same principles of practice. In fact (as Locke himself points out[14]) it is not possible to point to a set of practical principles which command universal assent. Nor are the difficulties made any less if, instead of a set of principles, a single principle such as that of maximising the general happiness is put forward.

2. *Acting on practical principles*

In addition to the problem of making sense of the idea of a faculty of moral sense or reason, there is a further difficulty. The original account of the mind was intellectualist in the sense that it offered an account of seeing which, in itself, was totally divorced from practice. Whatever our senses tell us about the way the world is, the question of how we are to behave in relation to it remains open. Behaviour can result only if desires are added. The account of practical principles now considered is intellectualist in the same way. Suppose for example that the early mill-owners saw that it was unjust to pay their workers so little while they themselves lived so well. (In view of the previous paragraph, 'saw' must be understood metaphorically here to mean something like 'came to realise'.) There is no reason to suppose that this would lead them to *do* anything to change matters unless they are credited also with a *desire* to do so. (It cannot be validly argued, as Mill seemed to think, that since each person desires his own happiness, everyone desires the happiness of all, that is the general happiness.[15]) The mere perception of the situation as unjust cannot lead to action without the addition of a desire for justice, any more than the perception of fruit on the bough can lead to its being picked unless there is also a desire for fruit. In other words, there is a gap between principles of practice and the practice to which they relate which can be bridged only by the introduction of the appropriate desires.

However, if men are to be credited with a desire to act in accordance with practical principles, some account must be given of how they come to have such desires. No such account readily presents itself. The desires to seek pleasure and to avoid pain do not seem to presuppose the prior acquisition of any ideas and they can therefore be presumed to be present from birth. But we cannot similarly be supposed to possess the desire to act on practical principles before we know what they are, and knowledge of them is acquired only after birth, through the use of moral sense or reason. So any suggestion that the desire to act on practical principles is innate is to be rejected. The most plausible suggestion is that we are so constituted that we acquire the desire to act on practical principles at the same time and in the same way as we come to know about them. But this gives reason, already suspect, a further job to do, once again without any indication of how it might be expected to do it. It also represents a major departure from the original story, according to which in finding out, for example, what a cat is, we do not at the same time come to like or dislike cats; our attitude to them is left completely open, to be settled only by consulting desires which are totally independent of how we suppose things to be. Nevertheless it is a departure which seems unavoidable.

3. *Alternative accounts*

The philosophical problems to which the account of practical principles outlined in this section give rise make it very unattractive. It is therefore worth considering whether any more acceptable account might have been given. Two possibilities will be considered.

The first is to regard practical principles (now called natural laws) as laws laid down by God for man's direction, laws which man, being God's creature, is by nature anxious to obey.[16] Philosophically this is not very different from the original account, practical principles now explicitly, rather than implicitly, having the status of a *deus ex machina*. This solution is in any case open only to religious believers. The second is to deny that practical principles do, after all, introduce any genuinely new element into the Lockean account. Such principles tell us only what, on reflection, is in our own interest from a long-term point of view, in contrast to what appears to be in our interest from moment to moment; they are really no more than principles of prudence. For example, it might be argued that the desire of the mill-owners considered earlier to improve the standard of living of their workers was based only on sound business principles: prosperous and happy workers are likely to work more efficiently than poor, unhappy ones. Such principles of prudence could be discovered through the use of reason, with no more now being meant by moral sense or reason than reflection on the means to be adopted to achieve our ends, and once discovered they need rely only on self-interest to influence behaviour. But this account can be attacked from both sides. Even those who are sympathetic to it must admit that many practical principles, such as honesty, do not on the face of it look like principles of prudence. Acceptance of them needs to be justified by showing, despite appearances to the contrary, that that is what they really are, for example by showing that honesty really does pay; and it is not obvious that this can be done. Those who are unsympathetic to it, on the other hand, will point out that what they are interested in is principles of practice which *cannot* be reduced to self-interest, and to deny the existence of such principles is hardly to provide a satisfactory account of them. To act honestly, for example, is to act honestly, whether it pays to do so or not. A combination of these points of view produces a demand for a justification of practical principles, combined with a refusal to consider any justification of the only kind which seems possible, one in terms of self-interest. There is therefore a persistent demand within the empiricist tradition for a justification of practical principles which cannot, in principle, be met. Since neither of these accounts of practical principles provides a viable alternative no further account will be taken of them.

4. The use to which practical principles are put
Finally, something must be said about the use to which Lockean principles might be put. Although it is already clear that their function is to guide behaviour, there is no obvious need for the guidance which they provide, since behaviour is already adequately based on self-interest. If they are to perform that

function, however, at least some individuals must be credited with a desire to act in accordance with them.

A distinction can be made between two sorts of behaviour and, correspondingly, between the practical principles needed to guide them. Behaviour may be personal in the sense that it is intended to change the circumstances either of the person himself or of other individuals. For example it might be said that in deciding what to do an individual should take into account not only his own interests but also those of others, in so far as they are likely to be affected. When principles are used in this way they may be referred to as moral principles. Behaviour may also be intended to change social rather than personal circumstances. Social circumstances, on this account, are said to be generated out of the unco-ordinated behaviour of rational individualists by the operation of impersonal mechanisms such as that of the market. The social or economic laws which govern the operation of such mechanisms presumably cannot themselves be changed but, provided they are understood, there may be some scope for changing the circumstances which result from their operation. Practical principles which draw attention to the way in which social circumstances should if possible be changed may be referred to as social principles.

Social principles function to guide behaviour which is intended to change social circumstances rather than affecting individuals directly, although the behaviour itself, like all behaviour, remains the behaviour of individuals. It must be assumed that the individuals whose behaviour is guided in this way not only know that there are such principles and desire to act in accordance with them but also that they possess the power to enable them to do so. The relevant knowledge and desire are likely to be confined to a minority although because of the realism of the Lockean position, it will be a minority that knows, or rather presumes itself to know, what is right. There will also be a need for knowledge of how to change things within the limits laid down by social laws, that is, for knowledge of the kind provided by the sciences of society, especially economics. It is likely also that the same minority will lay claim to both kinds of knowledge and will thus become the self-appointed high priests of social change.

The result will be a committed minority who wish to put

society right and who will seek the political power to enable them to do so. They will have no prejudice in favour of existing practice and will try to change it to make it conform to their *a priori* principles. Indeed since practical principles owe nothing to that practice they may seek to abolish it completely in order to make room for a new society planned as a whole from the start. Others will be expected to fit into a central plan rather than running their own affairs as they see fit, and local autonomy and personal responsibility will be replaced by central control and direction. This is a long way from the *laissez-faire* view that everything will work out for the best provided government interference is kept to the irreducible minimum, but the introduction of *a priori* practical principles makes a move in that direction almost inevitable.

VII. THE GOMBRICH ACCOUNT OF SOCIAL CRITICISM AND SOCIAL CHANGE

1. Are practical principles necessary?
The general line of the Lockean account of practical principles was dictated by the account of man and society which preceded it. The way in which men see the world depends directly on their individual experience of it, leaving the question of how they are to behave to be settled by further independent considerations. Men are rational individualists, pursuing only their own interests and employing whatever means happen to be available in order to do so. Social relations are entered into only in order to achieve pre-existing desires more efficiently and the social order which results in neither intended nor desired. Individual purposive action is sharply separated from the social context in which it takes place and social criticism can be based only on knowledge of *a priori* social principles which owe nothing to the social behaviour which it is their function to guide. Social principles, so understood, thus constitute what Professor Michael Oakeshott, in his inaugural lecture 'Political Education', calls a premeditated ideology.[17]

The Gombrich account does not make the same sharp contrast between man and society; from the beginning men are seen as members of society. The skills and techniques and ways of seeing which tradition provides are acquired from and shared with others. They are the shared possession of a community, not the private property of individuals. Moreover, the way in which experience is conceptualised is not neutral so far as possible action is concerned. The way of seeing which a tradition provides is also a way of doing; the related skills and techniques are not seen as neutral instruments to be used to satisfy whatever desires a particular individual may happen to have. The way we see the world, what we try to achieve in it and how we go about trying to do so are not independent of one another. We see and behave as we do primarily because we act in accordance with a way of seeing and doing laid down by a tradition and because people who belong to that tradition see and behave in that way. Tradition provides us with all the guidance we need. Hence there is no need to introduce *a priori* social principles to bridge the gap between neutral social facts and the value judgements which we may wish to make about them.

Practical principles were introduced into the Lockean account only because it was recognised that people might wish to criticise the social results of the uncontrolled behaviour of rational individualists and suggest ways in which things might be improved. Analogously, it must be recognised that people may also wish to criticise the guidance provided by tradition, although they will not wish to do so in all cases. The desire to criticise depends on awareness of the possibility of doing so. Without that awareness traditional ways of doing things (or, for that matter, the social order produced by the behaviour of individuals) will be seen as inevitable and will be accepted without question. A farming community, for example, may farm in the same way year after year, planting and harvesting the usual crops in the traditional way. It may also follow the same customs for the organisation of social life – family relationships, the ownership of property, the settlement of disputes and so on. In addition the community may do so without any realisation that things might be done differently and without having any conception of an alternative. At the present stage in man's social evolution such a failure of perception is likely to persist only in small, isolated communities which, lacking contact with others, are not presented with examples of ways of life different from their own. Traditions of this kind may be called tribalist. To stress the importance of tradition is not of course to recommend a return to tribalism. Indeed, if to do so were not paradoxical it would certainly be unrealistic: innocence, once lost, cannot be regained.

Tribal societies, in which there is no awareness of the possibility of criticising or rejecting traditional ways, can be contrasted with open societies in which there is such awareness. In relation to the latter a further distinction can be made between conservative traditions which consciously accept tradition as the best guide to the way to do things and critical traditions which favour criticism of existing ways with a view to their improvement. The most obvious example of such a tradition is of course post-seventeenth-century Europe. Both tribal and conservative traditions are similar in accepting uncritically the guidance provided by tradition, whereas critical traditions do not. Some account must therefore be given of the possibility of such criticism without relying on the *a priori* principles which were regarded as unsatisfactory in connection with the Lockean account.

To avoid possible confusion it should be pointed out that the Gombrich view, in being *philosophical*, is neutral as between conservative and critical traditions. Indeed a stress on the importance of tradition leads naturally to a taxonomy of traditions which recognises that traditions may be critical. The Lockean view, on the other hand, suggests that in deciding what to do we are faced with the blank sheet of infinite possibility and consequently that to allow ourselves to be bound by the past would be irrational. Although it cannot be said to favour critical traditions, since it ignores tradition altogether, it is in fact itself a critical tradition, the tradition known as utilitarianism.

2. *The Gombrich account of practical principles*

Reasons have been given for supposing that reliance cannot be placed on *a priori* practical principles in explaining the possibility of criticism of the guidance provided by tradition. Nevertheless, people constantly talk as though there were social principles, appeals to which are constantly made in arguments over social policy and in philosophical discussion. It is therefore necessary to give some account of what they are talking about.

According to the Lockean account, practical principles give

form and direction to practice; in fact without them there could not be said to be anything which could be called practice. The Gombrich view makes practice the primary reality, and a practice has no reality independently of its practitioners: the two are interdependent. Those who engage in a practice are guided by the way of doing which a tradition provides and the way of doing in turn exists only in the values and purposes of those guided by it. Thus practical principles are abstract but only in the sense that they are *abstracted from* practice. The particular purposes which men pursue are complex and various, as also are the traditions which guide them. It is therefore convenient and perhaps inevitable that attempts should be made to encapsulate their essence in abstract social principles and that as a result we should come to talk of freedom, equality, fraternity and so on. But talk of freedom, for example, arises only in the context of an awareness of a problem, such as the problem of choosing between different ways of institutionalising the relationship between the individual and central political authority. Talk of equality, again, is perhaps the product of a dream of material sufficiency, a by-product of the promise of endlessly increasing material prosperity offered by the industrial revolution. These examples are of course offered only by way of illustration; giving the full, true story of the origin of our ideas would be a matter for the historian of ideas rather than the philosopher. The point is that it is social practices which are the primary reality and social principles simply summarise, in abbreviated and highly abstract form, the way of doing which a practice contains and the ways in which people have thought it might be changed.

Suppose, for example, people say that society should become more egalitarian and we wish to get a clearer idea of what they actually have in mind in order to decide whether we agree with them. We cannot do so by asking what equality is, since there is no such thing, and it does not help much to ask what the word 'equality' really means. Rather we need to find out in what precise ways they are proposing that existing practice should be changed. Do they think that grammar schools should be replaced by comprehensive schools, that the public schools should be abolished, that all education should be taken over by central government, or what? Once we know what they are actually proposing it matters little whether they attempt to justify their proposal by appealing to an abstract principle of liberty, equality or anything else. What we do need to do is to consider what things would be like if the proposed changes were carried out and ask ourselves whether we would prefer our educational system or society to be like that. Of course we may know what kind of change has been recommended in the past under the banner of equality and therefore have some idea what to expect, but only in the vaguest and most general way. The suggestion that we should strive for a better, happier society, as the utilitarian claims, tells us even less. We need to know what counts as better or wherein happiness lies – whether in hi-fi in every car and television in every bedroom or in high-fibre diet, fresh air and meditation. In so far as we are in control of our destiny, we do not *have* to choose the one rather than the other, nor can it be shown, by abstract argument, that one choice rather than the other would be the correct choice and that to make any other choice would be to make a mistake.

In a nutshell, the Gombrich (or Oakeshott) view of practical principles is that they are abstract summaries of actual or proposed practice and cannot in themselves provide a practice with external guidance.

3. Social criticism and social change

(a) The problem stated
Practical social principles cannot function as external guides to practice or provide a basis for social change. However, if tradition provides our only guide how can tradition itself be criticised? How is a critical tradition – that is, a tradition of self-criticism – possible?

Criticism as understood in the present context must, as a matter of definition, be rational in the sense of providing grounds to which appeal can be made in argument. A tradition provides a way of seeing and doing which tells us what to do in differing circumstances; the guidance which it provides can be described, in very general terms, as telling us to do what we have always done. From the Lockean point of view such guidance is in itself worthless. According to that view, we should do what we did last time only if what we did last time was itself the right thing to do; and it was the right thing to do only if it was in accordance with the relevant *a priori* principle or principles. In the simplest and therefore preferred version reliance is placed on only one principle, the Principle of Utility, according to which we should pursue the greatest happiness of the greatest number. For example, suppose it is proposed to hang a man convicted of stealing a sheep. Then the question to be asked is whether to do so on this occasion (or to accept or continue to accept a rule laying this down as a general rule) would on balance result in an increase or a decrease in the general happiness. Past experience may be of help in answering *that* question since it is a straightforward question of fact, but in itself provides no guidance. The fact that those convicted of stealing sheep in the past have always been hanged is in itself irrelevant.

The Gombrich position is in effect the reverse of the Lockean. It is that the guidance provided by tradition neither can be nor needs to be supported by abstract principles which are external to it. Belief in abstract social principles is an illusion; tradition itself is our primary and in the final analysis our only guide. But in that case how is rational criticism of the guidance provided by tradition possible? What resources does a tradition possess which will allow it to change from within? Suppose tradition stipulates that a man convicted of stealing a sheep should be hanged but that certain individuals, who do not believe in abstract social principles, wish to criticise that tradition. How can they base their criticism on an appeal to tradition, since it is tradition which they wish to criticise?

(b) Criticism on grounds of efficiency

According to the account given earlier, traditions provide on the one hand skills and techniques and on the other ways of seeing and doing. There are therefore two elements in a tradition which, although they cannot be separated without artificiality, can each be considered in turn. As already noted, according to the Lockean account, to reason is to deliberate about the means to be adopted to achieve given ends, and there is no reason why the Gombrich account should not also recognise that there will be many situations in which there is agreement about what we want but disagreement about the most efficient way to get it. For example it may be agreed that it is desirable to teach children to read but there may be disagreement about the method which ought to be employed. It is also possible to assess and perhaps criticise the skill with which the method adopted is employed. Past practice also can be criticised from this point of view.

There is scope for criticism of skills and techniques within the context of a tradition, just as Lockean man employs his reason in order to find the most efficient way of achieving his objectives. There are, however, differences to be noted which considerably qualify this conclusion. First the Lockean account, neglecting as always the social dimension, tends to suggest that each individual employs his reason afresh to solve the problems which face him, as though no one else had ever faced similar problems before, and this is clearly false. But the view can easily be amended to take account of this. It was recognised by John Stuart Mill, for example, in his classic statement of the utilitarian position in *Utilitarianism* and dealt with by the authorisation of reliance on rules of thumb in order to avoid constant reference to the basic principle itself.[19]

Secondly, in the Lockean view, social principles are thought of as being objective and therefore the same at all places and at all times. For example in *Utilitarianism* Mill supposes that all who see the matter clearly will see that the Principle of Utility, or Greater Happiness Principle, provides the only possible standard of right and wrong. Once this is established the only scope for further disagreement is about means. As a result social criticism tends to be confined to the means to be used for the achievement of ends which, having already been settled once and for all, do not need to be discussed further. In the Gombrich view belief in the possibility of final agreement about ends is illusory. To revert to an example used earlier, there is no way of measuring and comparing the happiness which results from hi-fi and fast cars on the one hand and high-fibre diet and fresh air on the other in order to discover which is really most conducive to the general happiness. There will always be the possibility of disagreement and the need for discussion about ends. It is dangerously misleading to suppose that discussion can always be confined to questions about how to achieve given ends.

Thirdly, from the Lockean point of view means are in themselves neutral and can be assessed only for their efficiency.

But although the contrast between means and ends is useful, perhaps even indispensable, it is not always easy to maintain. Suppose, to revert to our earlier example, a man convicted of stealing a sheep is to be hanged; is hanging simply the (neutral) means to his execution or is the end intended not simply that he be executed but that he be hanged? Since courts always seem to fix the method of execution, the answer is probably the latter: shooting, for example, is a privilege reserved for soldiers. In that case the position is quite different from that of a murderer considering how best to dispose of his intended victim with the minimum risk of detection; from his point of view, any method will do provided it brings about the desired result safely. Thus the contrast between means and ends is always relative to situations and in any case is never absolute. In education, where things are more complex, the difficulty of distinguishing between means and ends is even greater. Can comprehensive schools really be thought of as the means to some other end, as sometimes seems to be supposed, such as a more egalitarian society? If so they can hardly be regarded as *neutral* means to that end, since children must spend years of their lives in them.

(c) Criticism of a tradition from without
The skills and techniques provided by a tradition can be criticised from a means-ends point of view, although with reservations. A way of doing, however, tells us not only *how* to do what we set out to do (through the provision of skills and techniques) but also *what* to do. How is that part of the guidance provided by tradition – the more important part – to be criticised? It will be convenient to distinguish between criticism of a tradition as a whole from without and criticism of it in part from within, even although there is great difficulty in deciding where one tradition ends and another begins, and to deal with these in turn.

There is a radical difference between the Lockean and Gombrich points of view of the possibility of criticism of a tradition as a whole. Since Lockean social principles are discovered through the use of moral sense or reason, independently of any actual practice, they provide a basis from which any actual tradition can be criticised and, moreover, can be criticised not simply in a qualified, partial way but as a whole.

Their supposed availability makes it possible to think of
constructing a new society or utopia from which the evils of the
past have been banished and in which everything is not only
new but also perfect. Not inappropriately the archetype for all
subsequent attempts to do so was God's plan of cleansing the
world of sin by the Flood; significantly, as we know, it failed to
do so. From the Gombrich point of view, the hope of building a
new world, like the belief in *a priori* practical principles which
inspired it, is a dangerous and destructive illusion. A tradition
can be criticised in its entirety only from the vantage point
provided by another tradition, that is, from outside; for
example, nineteenth-century Europeans regarded African
tribal society as primitive or savage. Such criticism can hardly
be regarded as rational in the sense indicated above, that is, in
the sense of having grounds to which appeal might be made in
argument with the other parties concerned, those living in a
tribal society. African traditions are *ex hypothesi* different from
European ones, and since Africans in being Africans are
committed to African rather than European traditions, no
appeal to European traditions can be expected to lead them to
see the error of their ways. Criticism need not be taken to justify
interference. Nevertheless, although not in that sense rational,
criticism can be made and may (though need not) be thought to
provide grounds for interference. If it is then conflict will result,
conflict which cannot, of course, be resolved by argument; what
happens will depend on the relative strength and vitality of the
traditions concerned.

The contrast between European and African traditions in the
nineteenth century is of course extreme; it is a contrast between
two different and incompatible ways of life, each of which was
complete in its own way. European painting, by contrast, has a
place in a larger context of European art and life which provides
a vantage from which it might be criticised without going
outside the total way of life to which it belongs. It might even be
totally rejected from the perspective provided by economic
practice, with its single-minded preoccupation with the profit
motive; Mr Gradgrind, for example, could be expected to see
little point in the painting of pictures unless there was a profit to
be made from their sale.

(d) Criticism of a tradition from within

Finally, some account must be given of the possibility of criticism of a tradition from within. This is where the real problem lies, as emphasised in (a) above. How is a critical tradition – that is, a tradition of self-criticism such as that of our own practice of teaching – possible if tradition itself provides the only guide?

The point of departure in this chapter was provided by Gombrich's perceptive remark that 'if art were only, or mainly, an expression of personal vision, there could be no history of art'. The inference taken there was that, since art does have a history, art cannot be only an expression of personal vision. The word 'only' is important, however. Gombrich is not denying that the artist may have a personal vision; rather he is asserting that something else is involved. I have argued that that something else is the way of seeing and doing provided by the tradition which guides the social practice of, for example, painting. What is needed now is an account of personal vision which is not only consistent with the emphasis already placed on the importance of tradition but which also allows us to see how a social practice and its traditions can be criticised and developed from within by its own practitioners on the basis of such a vision.

The history of painting is the story of the changes in ways of painting brought about by outstanding painters such as Giotto, Constable and Turner. It is most natural to speak of personal vision in talking about their achievements. Their work provides the landmarks in the history of painting because, in being fresh and new, it moved away from existing practice and was not, initially, shared by others. By definition such departures are exceptional and brought about only by exceptional people. All painters have a view about or vision of what they are doing but for most their personal vision is personal only in the sense that it is held by an individual person and is a vision only in the sense that it is a view about how the practice of painting should be carried out. There is no need for it to be different from that of other painters; initially, at least, it is bound to be similar, since it was acquired *from* others. In other words, to acquire a personal vision is in the first place to acquire the way of seeing which a tradition provides and, therefore, to become acquainted with and accept for oneself the overall point or purpose of a social practice such as painting or teaching. To do that is to acquire a view both of what that purpose is and what it ought to be. It is therefore to be in a position to justify or criticise what is done in that practice on a particular occasion by reference to that view.

To criticise a social practice from within is therefore to criticise the overall purpose of that practice and to do so by appealing not to something which is external to it, such as pleasure, but to that purpose itself. It is in effect an attempt to change the way its practitioners see their practice and hence also themselves and what they are doing, since it is its overall purpose which provides a practice with its principle of identity. Such criticism is possible only because the overall purpose of a social practice is not something fixed and given from outside, rather it depends on the individually held purposes of the many individuals who are its practitioners. Each has his own view of the purpose which he sees himself as sharing with others. And since individuals have varying histories, experiences and personalities, and will have been introduced to the practice in separate ways and had different experiences of it, it is easy to see that there is scope for some disagreement about what that purpose is.

The possibility of disagreement as such within a social practice is not difficult to explain. It was stipulated earlier that to count as being rational criticism must provide grounds to which appeal can be made in argument. It is possible for those who disagree about a social practice to appeal to such grounds only in so far as their disagreement is not total; that is, in so far as they not only disagree but also agree about its overall purpose. In the absence of any such agreement rational argument would be impossible. It is possible both to agree and disagree about the overall purpose of a social practice only because it is complex. There is nothing mysterious about the idea that a purpose may be complex and therefore that it is possible both to agree and disagree about it. For example, if two people agree that they would like to go for a nice day out together, it would still be possible for them to disagree about what counts as a nice day out. They may agree that they would like to go to the coast, but one would like to go where there are lots of people and shops whereas the other would like to go where there is peace and quiet and a good beach for swimming. Clearly they cannot have their day out together unless they reach some agreement, but there is scope for them to do so through rational argument. For example, one may suggest a place which has some nice shops but is also quiet and has a good beach. In the same way, there may be agreement about the overall purpose of teaching as the bringing about of education but disagreement about what counts as becoming educated. But in so far as they are part of the same social practice and share the same overall purpose, teachers can argue rationally about the relative importance of, for example, academic education in the narrow sense as compared with general social and emotional development. How radical it is possible to be – how far that is, it is possible to depart from what has previously been accepted without losing all intelligibility – will depend on a variety of factors. These will include, but will not be confined to, the personal appeal or charisma of those who offer their own vision of how things should be. In the context of teaching such a vision amounts to a philosophy of education. In the next chapter I will begin by distinguishing between *a* philosophy of education and *the* philosophy of education and will look briefly at some examples of the former.

CHAPTER 3. THE ORGANISATION OF EDUCATION

I. PHILOSOPHIES OF EDUCATION AND THE PHILOSOPHY OF EDUCATION

1. The difference between the *philosophy of education and a philosophy of education*

It has been suggested that teaching is a social practice guided by a social tradition which determines the way the teacher sees himself or herself and his or her role in the practice of teaching. Seeing depends on a way of seeing which is learnt from and shared with others; how we relate to the world in our practice similarly depends on a shared way of behaving or doing. To put it another way, both thought and action are structured by a conceptual scheme which is also reflected in the language which we use to talk about what we see and do; in so far as we use the same language and engage in the same social practices we also make use of the same conceptual scheme. It follows that there can be no coherent practice – whether of teaching, medicine or anything else – without a coherent conception of it on the part of its practitioners, although it need not be self-conscious or verbalised. If this is correct then it follows also that in order to change the way a practice is carried out – to change what is actually done – in a fundamental way it is necessary to change the conception of it which its practitioners have, and to change the central features of that conception, not just its details.

A philosophy of education may be thought of as an attempt to do this. It is likely to take the form of recommendations for practice rather than of an explicit suggestion that teachers should think of themselves and their task in some new way. Indeed it may take concrete form in the shape of a school run on new and original lines, thus offering an example for others to follow if they will. The new philosophy can then be transmitted both by visitors to the new school and descriptions of it, such as those of Summerhill provided by A. S. Neill. In order to count as a new philosophy the recommendations must rely on and introduce a new way of looking at things, for example a new conceptualisation of what constitutes a school and of the teacher's role in it. The introduction of a new philosophy of education is thus part of the practice of teaching, not something set apart from it, although forming part of its abstract periphery rather than of its practical core.

The academic philosopher is traditionally more detached from practice. If at all concerned with practice, he is likely to be interested only in understanding it rather than in changing it, and in doing so in the most general possible terms. Thus it was suggested in Chapter 1 that philosophy of education is concerned with our thinking about education rather than with education itself. It is now clear, however, that the way we think about our practice in educating is part of that practice, not something separate from it. (This is because education is a social phenomenon. By contrast the way we think about physical phenomena such as the weather or the waves or the nucleus of an atom *can* be sharply contrasted with the phenomena themselves.) It is therefore very difficult to maintain a distinction between *the* philosophy of education (the concern of the philosopher) and *a* philosophy of education (put forward by educational prac- titioners who are often, although misleadingly, referred to as educational theorists). It is difficult not only because how people think about a practice in which they are engaged and how they conduct themselves in it are connected, but also because there is no one way in which people think about the practice of teaching: there are many different practices carried on at various times and places and there is scope for difference even within the same practice. Any attempt to describe the practice of teaching is therefore bound to be not only highly general but also selective and to select is, if only implicitly, to criticise or recommend. Despite the difficulties, I prefer to retain the distinction between philosophy of education (or *the* philosophy of education) and *a* philosophy of education. The former is part of philosophy and is primarily concerned with understanding what education is rather than with how it should be carried on. The latter is part of educational practice and is primarily concerned with how education should be carried on, although its expression is bound to presuppose some view of what education is. The difference between them is purely one of emphasis and it is not always easy to decide whether a particular writer is offering the one or the other. Given that there is a difference, however, a brief outline of the point of view offered by three widely accepted philosophies of education would be appropriate at this point. The sketches which follow are intended to do no more than illustrate what is being talked about and there is no intention as such of either recommending or rejecting them. The views considered will be referred to as the traditional, progressive and radical views and each will be considered in turn.[1]

2. *Three philosophies of education*

(a) Traditional
The traditional view of education is subject- rather than child-centred with, at least in the early days, differences in attainment being attributed to wilfulness and wickedness. (Both Descartes and Locke, although not Plato, seem to have operated with the idea that, as Descartes puts it, 'good sense or reason, is by nature equal in all men'.[2]) Children are required to conform to a set pattern, those unable to do so being forced to drop out. Interest is centred on secondary and tertiary education, in the grammar school and university respectively, for the minority thought capable of benefiting from it, rather than on elementary or primary education in which all children share. The curriculum is well defined, emphasising the importance of basic skills (the three Rs) as the basis of the later study of traditional academic subjects. Organised games are important, but only as a means of letting off steam and training character. Teaching methods are formal – lecturing and talking – with detailed direction which leaves little to the initiative of the child; there is much emphasis on competition and consequently on examinations and achievement. The social structure is authoritarian, the authority of the teacher being backed by a system of punishment which may include corporal punishment. Education is viewed as heteronomous in having a social function, whether it be that

of providing a literate workforce or army, or home or colonial rulers. It is therefore desirable that education should be appropriate to future social, economic and political circumstances. An autonomous view of education may, however, be taken for the elite minority who go to university, though not, perhaps, for those who go to polytechnics. Education is admittedly socially devisive, with second-class educational provision, perhaps of a practical or technical kind, for working-class and less bright children. Finally there is a commitment to a principle of liberty, allowing parents freedom of choice, within their means, of the education they want for their children and giving the more able children the opportunity to compete for free access to educational resources. Correspondingly, importance is attached to the quality of education received by the few rather than to fairness in its distribution.

(b) Progressive
The progressive view of education is child-centred, stressing the need to learn about children and the way they grow and develop if they are to be taught effectively. Attention is paid to the earlier stages of education, including nursery education, and young children are presented as enquiring and co-operative. The curriculum is less strictly tied to academic subjects and caters for artistic and emotional as well as cognitive development. Teaching methods are informal and based on knowledge of children, making use of their interests and allowing them to find things out for themselves in a structured environment. Ideally teaching methods are tailored to individuals and reflect a caring attitude to children as children and as individuals. Education is viewed as autonomous in the sense of being for the benefit of those being educated, not for any external purpose, and all children have the right to benefit from it. An imperialist view is taken of the function of the teacher, the result not only of a tender-minded concern for the child but also of a perception of the connection between the child's ability to benefit from education and its general welfare and home environment. Finally there is a commitment to an egalitarian principle leading to a rejection of separate educational provision for different sections of society.

(c) Radical
The radical view of education is more stridently and overtly political than either of its predecessors. There is a rejection of any sharp distinction between children and adults. Children are regarded as autonomous and should be given responsibility for their own education rather than having it imposed on them by authority. There is a consequent rejection of any fixed curriculum in favour of diversity and choice. The individual is to make his own way in the world rather than being dictated to by an alien bureaucracy. There is a further rejection of the school as an institution staffed by trained professionals employing teaching methods acquired during special training. Not only is the authority of the teacher and his coercive role rejected, so also is the caring, friendly attitude of the progressive teacher, such attitudes now being labelled 'sentimental' or 'covert manipulation'. Education is thought of as being for the benefit of the individual rather than of society or the state, and should always be related to what the person acquiring it currently wants for himself.

(d) What a philosophy of education is
The three philosophies of education described could each be said to offer a different way of looking at the practice of teaching. Each tends to be offered as a package, the parts of which are, or are thought to be, mutually supporting. They tend to see each other as rivals and, since each is held with passion and commitment, to be strongly critical of each other. Each offers a cluster of views about the nature of the child, the curriculum, teaching method, the social structure of teaching, the relation between education, the individual and society, and the scope of the teacher's job, together with an attitude to the distribution of educational advantage and class division in society. Each tends to be associated with a more general political and social point of view – conservative, liberal and extreme right or left wing. Each approach tends to be held self-consciously and to refer back, like religions, to messianic figures such as Plato, Rousseau, Froebel, Piestalozzi, Rudolph Steiner, and more recently A. S. Neill and Ivan Illich. In short, each tries to articulate and either to reassert or modify the direction of traditional ways of carrying

out the practice of teaching, although not all would perhaps be happy with that definition.

A philosophy of education is primarily an attempt to articulate or change the way in which those engaged in the practice of teaching conceptualise themselves and their practice. Each of the views sketched above offers a set of proposals linked by its own preferred conception of the child, the role of the teacher and the relation between the individual and society. Each package is backed by claims to moral, psychological and philosophical insights, although these are often so deeply embedded in the conceptualisation of the practice that it is difficult or impossible to isolate them for separate examination and assessment. None compels rational acceptance, indeed each inevitably begs the question in its own favour in putting forward its own case, inviting commitment rather than rational conviction. This should not be surprising in view of the arguments put forward in the previous chapter against the possibility of any neutral assessment of the merits of the ways of looking at things provided by competing traditions. A practice involves not only a way of looking at things but also a way of doing which reflects a shared set of values; and the view that there are educational or any other values which can be discovered *a priori* by philosophers of education or educational theorists or, indeed, by anyone else, and which must therefore be accepted by all, has already been rejected. Values exist only in being held; they are not part of Locke's independently existing reality of things.

II. TEACHING AS A PROFESSION

1. *Teaching as organised bureaucratically*
All three philosophies of education considered in the previous section take the adequacy of the teacher-pupil model of teaching for granted. Consequently, although I have suggested that a philosophy of education is itself part of the practice of education, none show much recognition of the fact that teaching is a social practice or attach much importance to views about how that practice should be organised. (The radical view perhaps should be credited with the negative view that it should be *dis*-organised and so constitutes a kind of exception.) However,

different views about how this should be done are possible. This can be brought out by contrasting what I will call the bureaucratic and the professional points of view. My own preference is that as far as possible teaching should be organised along professional rather than bureaucratic lines, and expressing and articulating such a preference comes close to offering a further philosophy of education. In the course of doing this I hope to draw attention to features which must be features of any social activity, however organised. What I call responsibility for purpose must be located somewhere, for example, though it need not be located in the doctors, teachers and so on who engage in face-to-face relations with patients and children.

From the Lockean point of view, teaching is not the name of a practice at all, it is simply the name of a transaction, of a kind made explicit by the teacher-pupil model, between individuals. The parties to such transactions, most importantly the teachers, are rational individualists acting independently of other such individualists. However, if we look at education it is clear that it forms a system and some account must be given of how this comes about; why, for example, many different teaching transactions tend to be concentrated at roughly the same time and place, in other words in schools. This of course is simply a particular instance of the general Lockean problem of how, given the original account of men as rational individualists, social order can emerge. Economic order is plausibly explained as the result of the actions of individuals, each acting as an individual, which are nevertheless co-ordinated through the mechanism of the market. It has been noted, however, that the results of the uncontrolled operation of market forces may be thought undesirable, for example if they lead to great inequality of income, widespread unemployment, industrial disease and so on. Recognition of this leads to the introduction of practical principles, the function of which is to guide the actions of those who take it upon themselves to put things right. Those who also have the power to act in this way may be called bureaucrats. Educational services can be bought and sold like any other service or commodity but it is now widely regarded as unsatisfactory to leave educational provision to the unhindered operation of market forces. The existence of a free educational system can only be explained from the Lockean point of view as the result of the activity of bureaucrats. These are likely to be local or central government officials and politicians who may, although not necessarily, derive their power from democratic voting procedures. Bureaucrats do not see themselves as part of the systems they organise and make use, or purport to make use, of *a priori* practical principles acquired independently of them in doing so. For that reason they may appear alien to those whom they organise.

There is no doubt that education is to some extent organised from outside in this way and good reason to suppose it will continue to be, since most of the very large sums needed to finance it come from public funds. There is also no doubt that those who believe in the existence of *a priori* practical principles of the kind discussed in the previous chapter, and believe also that they have access to them, think that education should be organised in this way; but it is also possible that it might be organised to a greater or lesser extent along professional lines. I would like to offer an exploration of that possibility.[3]

2. Teaching as a profession

(a) Payment
A professional is, minimally, one who makes his living as, for example, a wrestler, footballer or tennis player, in contrast to an amateur who carries out the same activities but does not depend upon them for a livelihood. Teachers are normally professionals in this sense, irrespective of whether the practice of teaching is organised bureaucratically or as a profession; but a professional in this limited sense is not necessarily a member of a profession in the fuller sense to be developed below.

(b) Knowledge and skills
There is an obvious connection between membership of a profession and the possession of special knowledge and skills, and the prestige and regard which comes with it, especially when it is used to help others in direct face-to-face contacts. Those who wish to enter a profession must show that they possess the required knowledge and skill by passing examinations and qualifying in other ways for entry into that profession. (Examinations may also be used to restrict entry to a profession through

limiting the number of those admitted for training by adjusting the pass standard. But in so far as a so-called professional body acts in such a way it acts as a trade union rather than as a profession.)

Professions differ greatly in the kind and extent of the knowledge and skill which they involve. Medicine clearly involves a great deal of specialised knowledge and skill and perhaps for that reason is commonly thought to provide the best example of a profession, but it would be wrong to suppose that all professions must follow the same pattern or that they should be judged by the standard set by medicine. It would be a mistake, for example, to expect the practice of the church to be based on scientific discoveries in the same way as medical practice. Not all professions depend to the same extent or in the same way for their claim to professional status on their possession of specialised knowledge and skills. Moreover, an applicant's possession of them, even if undisputed, would not necessarily be sufficient to guarantee that such a claim would be accepted. The most central features of a profession have yet to be discussed. The question of how far teaching depends on the possession of specialised knowledge and skills will be discussed in section 3.

(c) Responsibility and purpose

In this subsection I will distinguish between the notions of responsibility as agent, social responsibility, a responsible person and responsibility for purpose.

Responsibility as agent The most important aspects of a profession, from the point of view of the organisation of a practice, centre around the notions of responsibility and purpose. The Gombrich account, elaborated in the previous chapter, is an account not only of seeing but also of doing; the painter not only sees the world in a certain way but also presents the world as seen in that way to others through his paintings. This involves the transformation of an originally blank surface into a picture of, for example, Flatford Mill, a transformation for which the painter can be said to be responsible in the sense that he brought it about or made it happen. More generally, people may be said to be the authors or agents of their own actions in the sense that their actions originate with them. What happens when they act happens because they choose to make it happen, knowing what they are doing and being aware of the possibility of acting otherwise. They can therefore be said to be *responsible as agent* for what happens as a result of their actions.

Social responsibility   It is only because people are responsible for the changes which their actions bring about that it makes sense to assess their actions by reference to standards which lay down what they ought to do, whether those standards are thought of as provided by tradition or as *a priori* Lockean principles. It also makes sense to ask them to explain or clarify their actions, in other words to give an account of themselves, in order to allow comparisons to be made between what they in fact do and what they ought to have done or refrained from doing. People may therefore be held *socially responsible* or accountable for what they do, that is, what they are responsible for in the basic, agency sense.

A responsible person   Responsibility in the agency sense is basic to any conception of morality, since we can be held socially responsible, or accountable, only for what is under our control. There is, however, a further notion, that of a responsible person, which is of more direct relevance to the idea of a profession. A responsible person is one who does what he should simply because he sees that he should. There is no need either for someone else to see that he does what he should or for any other form of external pressure such as a system of sanctions or rewards. In the sphere of employment, acceptance of personal responsibility is more likely where there is scope for the worker to take pride in his work because, for example, he is able to see the finished product and to see in it a reflection of his own skill. It is also preferable, both from the point of view of efficiency and of the worker's own self-respect. Moreover, close supervision becomes increasingly impracticable when specialised knowledge and skill are required, as they typically are in the case of a profession.

Responsibility for purpose   Part of the definition of a profession which is being developed is that the members of a profession should be responsible persons. Closely connected with this requirement, there is a further connection between the idea of a profession and what will be called *responsibility for purpose*. In order to explain what is meant by this a distinction will be made between a principal and one who merely acts as an agent for another. Normally people employ others because they want something done but, for one reason or another, cannot or do not wish to do it themselves and they therefore employ someone else to do it for them. The employee may then be said to be no more than the agent of his employer, on whose behalf he acts. No purpose of his own is reflected in what he does, apart from the wish to be paid; he becomes, for the period of his employment, simply an agent-for-another. A principal, on the other hand, acts in his own right; he is his own agent, not simply an agent-for-another. An agent-for-another, if he is a responsible person, may accept responsibility for achieving the ends or purposes towards which his actions are directed. A principal, on the other hand, accepts responsibility not merely for achieving but also for setting the ends of his actions. It is his purposes which are reflected in what he does and not merely those of others, and it is central to the idea of a profession that its members accept responsibility for purpose in this sense. The distinctive purpose which, above all, makes the profession the profession it is (for example, the medical profession, the teaching profession) is primarily provided by its members rather than imposed on them by any external authority.

In the final analysis, in relation to any practice, whether it is organised as a profession or bureaucratically, somebody must be responsible not only for seeing that things go well but also for providing the overall sense of purpose or direction without which nothing would count as successful. A profession is no more than a special case of a practice guided by a social tradition, and a tradition can guide a practice only if the guidance which it offers is freely accepted by someone, that is by someone who accepts its purpose as their own. If a practice is organised as a profession, responsibility for purpose must be diffused throughout its membership. In the case of the caring professions, which include medicine and social work as well as teaching, this means primarily those who engage in the face-to-face contacts with patients, clients and pupils which lie at its core: the doctor who has patients and is not simply an administrator, the social worker who has a case load, and of course the teacher who spends his day at what is sometimes called the chalk face. If a practice is organised bureaucratically, responsibility for purpose need be accepted only by a small number of people who may not take any part in the day-to-day life of the practice and may be active only in an administrative capacity. If the Gombrich account is accepted, in both cases the way in which that responsibility is exercised will depend on a way of doing provided by a tradition, although the people concerned, especially if they are bureaucrats, may themselves describe what they are doing as relying on Lockean practical principles of the kind discussed earlier. As also suggested earlier, those who believe in the existence of *a priori* practical principles – and such is the influence of Locke on our intellectual tradition that belief in them is widely regarded as the only alternative to cynicism – are likely to think that the organisation of education should be left to those who have access to them and therefore know how things should be done. Indeed they are unlikely to be able to form any idea of how else it could be organised. Paradoxically, Locke joins forces with Plato at this point, in effect endorsing a position close to the central Platonic doctrine that only philosophers, who alone know what form the state – or education – should take, should be kings.

(d) The professional ideal of service
Professional purposes are distinguished as such in two ways: first, they concern the interest of others and, secondly, they concern some special aspect of the interests of others.

The interests of others   It is an important part of the idea of a profession that a member of a profession, although acting as a principal and therefore according to purposes of his own, also acts in the interests of persons other than himself. He can therefore be said to be motivated by an ideal of service to others. A metaphor commonly used to express this idea, for example in both the *Republic* and the *New Testament*, is that of the good shepherd who guards and cares for his flock. Similarly, the teacher is concerned about the welfare of the children he teaches and acts primarily in their interests rather than in his own or those of his employer. It is obvious, however, that the shepherd is not *just* concerned with the welfare of his flock, since sheep are kept for the sake of their meat and wool. In the same way, it must be recognised that teachers also have interests of their own – to earn a living, to achieve advancement in their profession, and so on – and that they also have a contractual duty to their employer, and consequently that the interests of those taught, self-interest and duty to employer may on occasion conflict. This is just a fact of life, which does not show that teachers are indifferent to the interests of the children they teach; indeed, a reason commonly given for choosing a career in teaching is the desire to do a worthwhile job.

It is sometimes denied that disinterested action in this sense is possible, since people in acting freely always do what they want. But although this is true, it is a truth about what it means to be a responsible agent in the sense introduced earlier. The action of an agent originates with the agent in the sense that he chooses to make what happens happen, knowing what he is doing and of the consequences of doing it and aware of the possibility of acting otherwise. It is in this sense that in acting freely people always do what they want. But this tells us nothing about what people want or whether what they want is concerned with their own interests or those of others. Of course there is no reason why people should not do many things which are in their own interests, but there is no *a priori* reason why *all* of the things which they do should be.

The special aspect of the interests of others Professions differ from one another primarily in the aspect of the interests of others which they are particularly concerned to promote and which thus defines their distinctive professional purpose, in other words they differ in their overall purpose. Thus the teaching profession is concerned with education, the medical profession with health, the clergy with spiritual welfare and so on. Each of the professions also has its specialised knowledge and skills, as discussed earlier, which makes it well placed to provide help of the relevant kind. Professional concern is therefore for the most part implicit in professional practice rather than expressed explicitly, although attempts may be made to articulate the nature of that concern. A natural way of describing such attempts would be calling them attempts to express the philosophy of the profession concerned.

(e) The unity of a profession

A member of a profession acts as a principal rather than as an agent-for-another; it is therefore his purposes which are reflected in what he does rather than those of others. However, the unity of a profession depends on the fact that its members not only individually adopt professional purposes but in doing so adopt the same purposes. In addition, they not only share the same purposes but are also aware of doing so, and it is this awareness of common purpose, and of the possession of the knowledge and skill needed to pursue it, which gives a profession the sense of identity on which its unity depends.

The members of a profession form a social group with a distinct identity primarily because they see themselves as forming a group; if they did not *see* themselves in this way then they would not *in fact* be a group. As it is each not only sees himself as a member of that group but he also sees others as members, and as members like himself. He thus not only sees himself in that way but also sees others as seeing him in the same way. Each therefore is aware not only of his own membership and of the membership of others, but also of the awareness of others of his membership and of his awareness of theirs. The members of a social group are thus related to one another by what I will call the relation of reciprocal self-awareness, and it is their being related in this way that brings a social group such as a profession into existence. The group which they form is therefore a group in a very special sense and is an example of what will be called a primary social group. Primary social groups depend for *being* what they are – for their reality – on being *seen* as what they are. They really do exist but only in their own way, which is different from that of physical objects such as tables and chairs. Tables and chairs, we suppose, exist independently of our perception of them; our seeing them does not bring them into existence, and they do not cease to exist when we see them no longer. This is true also of groups or classes of physical objects and indeed of people classified on the basis of their physical characteristics; for example, the class of all the books on my desk at this moment or all the red-headed people who live in this town. Primary social groups do not belong to a reality which is independently given in this sense, but they do belong to their own kind of social reality. Thus although the claim that reality as such is a construction of the human mind was rejected in the previous chapter, that claim is true if made of *social* reality.[4]

One respect in which a profession is a special case of a primary social group will be considered in the next subsection. Meanwhile it is worth pointing out that it is not difficult to see how the members of a profession might come to make the overall purpose of a profession their own and thus come to share a common purpose. A recruit to a profession might be attracted by what he knows its purposes to be and in the course of professional training he will come to understand more clearly what those purposes are and to adopt them as his own. Indeed an important part of professional training is coming to think and feel like a member of that profession; one who fails to do so is unlikely to remain in the profession. This may be recognised in the provision of special courses, for example in the history and philosophy of education, but need not be, since the ethos of a profession is likely to be reflected in everything which is done, for example, in a college of education or a teaching hospital or, indeed, in the normal practice of the profession.

A sociologist, in considering the professions, might emphasise the way in which they seek to reinforce their sense of separate identity by wearing distinctive dress, eating together or taking part in elaborate ceremonies. But there would be no point in their behaving in that way unless they already saw themselves as having a distinct identity which they wished to preserve and strengthen. Details of this sort will not therefore be considered further.

(f) Recognition and autonomy

Recognition   A profession forms a social group in the sense that its members see themselves and each other as a profession, but the group which they form can constitute a profession only within and as part of a larger social group which I will call a community. That this is the case is implicit in much of what has been said already, for example that professional purposes relate to the interests of others. A group does not constitute a profession unless it is seen as a profession not only by its own members but also by the rest of the community. In other words, it is necessary to be recognised as a profession in order to be a profession.

Public recognition is thus essential to being a profession, not something external to it. It have tried to draw attention to the factors on which such recognition might rationally be based under the headings of knowledge and skill, responsibility and purpose, the professional ideal of service and a sense of unity. But recognition is something additional to these and does not follow automatically when they have been achieved. However deserving in other respects, a group of people cannot be a profession unless they are publicly recognised as a profession. Thus what might be called orthodox medicine is a profession but unorthodox medicines such osteopathy, chiropractice and acupuncture may not be. (This may be the result of trade union rather than professional activity on the part of the medical profession, but if so it is an activity primarily aimed at the prevention of public recognition.)

Autonomy   Recognition as a profession bears important consequences: in granting recognition the community is in effect accepting the profession's own view of itself as being both able and willing to offer something which the public needs. It may consequently be prepared to finance the profession's activities out of public revenue. It may also agree that the profession's willingness to accept responsibility makes external supervision less necessary. The profession may therefore be granted automomy, its own members being seen as the people best qualified and motivated to organise their professional activities. Autonomy is therefore a further characteristic of a profession. Other things, such as greater financial reward and higher social status, may come with prosperity but need not, and are of more sociological than philosophical interest.

(g) The place of a profession in the community
As pointed out above, the members of a profession form a social group only as part of a larger community and professional purposes relate not only to the interests of individuals but also to those of the community itself. (Literacy, health and so on are public goods, just as ignorance, disease and crime are social problems.) It was also suggested that in order to be a profession, a group of people must be seen as a profession by the rest of the community.

The *ideas* of a profession and a community reflect this aspect of the relation between a profession and the community to which it belongs. The idea of a profession is of something which is a part of a larger whole, whereas the idea of a community is of something which, although complex in that it consists of parts, has a completeness or wholeness which its parts lack. There are many examples of ideas which can be contrasted in this way; for example, the ideas of a segment of an orange and of an orange, the ideas of a bodily organ such as an eye or heart and of the animal body to which it belongs, and the ideas of a carburettor and of a complete motor car. Part of what is involved in picking some things out as having a completeness which others lack is the thought that they are independently viable, whereas the others are not. A motor car can provide transport, whereas a part of a car such as a carburettor by itself cannot. Similarly, an animal can survive, whereas an isolated organ cannot. In the same way a community is complete in that it offers its members an independently viable way of life, whereas a profession can make only a contribution to such a life.

Each profession makes its own distinctive contribution to the life of the community. The teaching profession, with its special concern for education, tries to enrich and give deeper meaning to the lives of individuals. It also makes a more explicitly social contribution. A society provides the framework within which its members live, a framework which is largely independent of the individuals who happen to be its members at any particular time. They are born into it and it survives their deaths, for although it would cease to exist if it no longer had any members, those who die are replaced by succeeding generations. But although new members are born into it, they can make no contribution to its survival until they acquire a social identity. They do this through interacting with and thus becoming part of their social environment; they are then themselves available to influence later generations in the same way. If a society is to survive, this process must be carried out efficiently, and if the society has a rich cultural and intellectual tradition this cannot be left to chance. It is an important part of the purpose of the teaching profession to see that it is not.

A profession can make a contribution to the life of the community because the values which its purpose reflects are also more general social values. Only the medical profession is *professionally* concerned with health but health is of concern to us all. Only the teaching profession is *professionally* concerned with education but education is widely valued by others. Indeed, if this were not the case the rest of the community would have no motive for recognising a profession as a profession or for financing its activities. It follows that the particular social value with which a profession is concerned will be only one of a number of such values in the community. The values of a community form a system which relates to every aspect of the way of life provided by that community and has the same kind of completeness as a community itself. Different social values therefore support rather than compete with one another; the relation between them is primarily that of complementarity. For example, material prosperity is valued for its own sake and is also a means to health, education and so on and, conversely, health and education make prosperity more possible.

Social values may also compete, in the sense that the pursuit of one may lead to the neglect or even the rejection of others. For example, prosperity may lead to the so-called diseases of affluence, education may lead to a contempt for trade and industry, and so on. More importantly, the pursuit of human purposes normally makes demands on resources which are scarce in relation to the demands made upon them, so that resources used in one way are not available to be used in others. For example, land used for a hospital cannot also be used for a school, or to grow crops, or as a park. From this point of view, a profession may be thought of as a kind of custodian or guardian of a part of the community's stock of values. Although its view is partial, it is held with a commitment and backed by a knowledge which others cannot be expected to share. It can therefore be expected to do its best to make sure that a fair share of the community's resources is allocated to its own area of interest. What counts as a fair share will depend on a view of the value system as a whole, including some conception of the relative importance of its parts, and in the end, on a view about how life as a whole should be lived in the community concerned.

3. Is teaching a profession?

I have suggested that teaching is a social activity which may be organised either bureaucratically or as a profession, and have tried to spell out the latter suggestion in more detail. Two questions present themselves at this point: is teaching in fact a profession? and should teaching be a profession? I will try to say a little about each of these in turn.

The question 'is teaching a profession?' can be answered, if at all, only if understood as a question about teachers at a particular place and time, for example about teachers in England towards the end of the nineteenth century, teachers in Australia today, teachers in Greece at the time of Socrates and Plato, teachers in Rome under the emperor Nero, and so on. All presumably tried to bring about learning in others through face-to-face contacts with them, otherwise we would have no grounds for calling them teachers. However, this tells us little or nothing about how they were organised. There is no reason to expect that what is true of one is true of another. The question whether teaching is a profession can be answered only by consulting the relevant facts in each case. No general answer is possible.

The trouble is that the relevant facts are bound to be both complex and inaccessible. For example, if a particular group of teachers form a profession they will be motivated by an ideal of service. But it is always difficult to answer questions about other people's motives when we are often unclear about our own. Moreover in view of the advantages which recognition as a profession brings, reliance cannot be placed on what people *say* their motives are. Similar considerations can be expected to apply to questions about how people see themselves and are seen by others.

Again, the various features of a profession to which attention has been drawn are not equally relevant in all cases. It would be unreasonable, for example, to expect church practice to be based on knowledge of scientific principles in the same way as medical practice is, and the position of teaching in this respect (to be discussed later in section III.2) is contentious and at best unclear. No final decision can be made about whether teaching is a profession without first deciding on the weight to be attached to the many different factors involved and there is bound to be disagreement about how to do that. There is certainly no one correct way of doing this, even if the proposed definition of a profession is accepted. Furthermore, although according to that definition it is *necessary* for the members of a profession to see themselves and be seen by others *as* a profession, it is by no means *sufficient*. It would be naïve in the extreme to suppose that all of those groups traditionally regarded as professions conform to all of the requirements laid down by the definition.

Even if all these difficulties could be overcome, there is no reason to expect that a clear, unambiguous answer to the question whether a particular group of teachers were a profession would be available. It would be wholly unrealistic, for example, to expect all teachers, without exception, to be responsible persons for whom any form of supervision was unnecessary, or to expect all of them, all the time, to be motivated solely by an ideal of service. Similarly, a profession has to be recognised as a profession and is accordingly allowed to run its own affairs without outside interference. But the public may not be unanimous in granting recognition; even if they were, they would be unlikely to wish to leave education wholly in the hands of the teaching profession, or for that matter to leave health solely in the hands of the medical profession, defence in the hands of the military, and so on.

In view of the difficulties in establishing the facts, it is fortunate that it is not really necessary for us to be able to say whether teaching is or is not a profession. The point of offering an account of a profession is to draw attention to one way in which teaching might be organised and therefore to draw attention to something which might be aimed at or, in so far as already achieved, defended. This brings us to the second question referred to above, whether teaching *ought* to be a profession.

4. *Should teaching be a profession?*

According to the account given in section VII.2 of the previous chapter, social principles do no more than summarise in an abstract way the guidance provided by a tradition. They cannot themselves offer any independent guidance. It would therefore hardly be helpful to appeal to abstract social principles in support of the claim that teaching should be a profession. The best way of defending such a claim would be by describing what it would be like for teaching to be a profession, which I have already tried to do, but perhaps something more can be said to bring the issue into focus.

Although I have argued that teaching must be thought of as a social activity, I have also pointed out that different views are possible about how the practice of teaching might be organised. That teaching should be a profession is therefore no more than one possibility among others although it could be argued that any form of social organisation must possess the features to which I have drawn attention in offering an account of a profession. Social life of any kind is possible only because people are agents and therefore capable of acting. Since they act, they can be held socially responsible or accountable for what they do. Moreover, however things are organised, if they are organised at all, *someone* must accept responsibility for seeing that they go well: if not the individual worker or practitioner, then whoever is appointed to supervise him, and if not the supervisor, then whoever makes sure that the supervisor does his job. To paraphrase the words of a recent American president, the buck must stop somewhere. Again, someone's purpose must be involved in what is done; we cannot all be agents-for-another all the time. Somebody must accept responsibility for purpose, if not the teaching profession, then the bureaucrats or politicians must do so. Moreover, even if these are not features which all forms of social life must possess, they would be features of any which we would choose, since taken together they amount to little more than a definition of social rationality. For example, although we do not have to base our social practices on whatever knowledge and skills are available, it is reasonable to suppose that we would wish to do so.

Nevertheless, the suggestion that teaching should be a profession does point to one possibility among others and is likely to be contentious. This is because what has been put forward is a package, the parts of which are mutually supporting, like the parts of the philosophies of education described at the beginning of this chapter; what makes that package contentious is not so much the features which form its contents as the way they are put together. The features themselves can be divided into two groups: those which precede recognition (including those discussed under the headings of knowledge and skill, responsibility and purpose and ideal of service) and those which follow from it (discussed under the heading of recognition and its consequences). Recognition itself, which does not belong to either group, does not follow automatically from the features on which it might rationally be based, those in the first group. But if granted it does bring the principle feature of the second group, autonomy, with it. It is this which makes the idea of a profession contentious. Presumably no one is likely to object to teachers possessing the features in the first group but it does not follow that everyone will agree to their becoming autonomous. In order to see why this might be so I will consider what autonomy involves.

The most natural context in which to talk about autonomy is when talking about a sovereign state or nation such as France, West Germany or the United Kingdom. A state is described as autonomous if it has the right to conduct its own affairs in its own way without external interference. It is less natural to speak of individual people as autonomous but we do talk about treating them as adults, and to treat a person as an adult is to allow him also, subject to clearly defined limits, to conduct his own affairs in his own way. Similarly when people associate together for limited purposes there is a presumption that they too should be allowed, within limits, to conduct the affairs of the associations which they form in their own way. In each case it is understood that the rights concerned are limited in certain ways. States do not have the right to interfere in the internal affairs of other states. Adults have the right to conduct their own affairs only in so far as in doing so they do not interfere with the right of others to do the same or, more generally, break the law; and similarly for associations of adults. The problem where a profession is concerned is that although its purposes are admittedly its own, they are of their very nature not exclusively its own, since they concern the interests of other people, and if those people are to be treated as adults who have a right to run their own lives, they must as far as possible be allowed some say in how their interests are to be served.

How far it is possible to allow a profession's clients a say in how their interests are to be served depends on whether we are thinking of them as individuals or as a group. There is some scope for consultation between individual members of a profession and clients in face-to-face situations, although how much depends on the profession concerned and the exact situation. A doctor usually knows, at least in general, what his patient wants; the problem is how best to achieve it, and that may depend on technical medical knowledge. Teachers mostly teach children who are required by law to go to school but there is some scope for consulting them or their parents about their school career. What is done will in any case have to be done within the constraints set up by the way in which medical or educational practice as a whole is organised.

A profession's clients and potential clients considered as a group include everyone who might from time to time stand in need of expert professional help, and in effect that means the community as a whole. The question then is how far the community, as a whole or in part, can have a say in the organisation of medical, educational and other practices. If those practices are organised as professions, then they will run themselves; if they are not, then somebody else, civil servants, will have to be appointed to do so bureaucratically. Civil servants, at least in theory, act on behalf of the government and in a democracy the government is freely elected. There is therefore a justification, if only of a tenuous kind, for allowing bureaucrats to run education: they are no more than the agents of the community as a whole and what they do simply reflects the will of society. Either way, somebody must be trusted with the power to run things. The case for trusting that power to a profession is the case for trusting it to those who know and care most about the things concerned.

Finally, it was pointed out earlier that people are held socially responsible, or accountable, for what they choose to do, especially when acting as principals rather than as agents-for-others. In so far as it is autonomous, a profession is therefore fully responsible in this sense for what it does. In the next chapter I will consider what is meant by accountability.

III. WHAT THE TEACHER NEEDS TO KNOW

1. The theory of education[5]
I have suggested that teaching is best thought of as a social

activity which may be organised either as a profession or bureaucratically. However it is organised, the question arises as to what those engaged in it are to do and how they are to go about it. The first question concerns the overall purpose of teaching; the second concerns the means which are to be adopted in order to achieve that purpose.

Detailed answers to these questions are provided by the tradition in accordance with which the activity of teaching is carried on and, since different traditions provide different answers, no detailed account of the guidance provided can be given without a detailed study of the tradition concerned. At a more abstract level, something can be said in general about the kind of overall purpose which an activity must have if it is to be characterised as an activity of teaching; in a word, its purpose must be that of bringing about education. Accordingly an account of education will be offered in a later chapter. Similarly, something can be said in a general way about the kind of knowledge and skills which might be made use of in pursuing that purpose, and I will try to do that later in this section.

First, some account must be given of what is widely known as the theory of education. In relation to the practice of teaching, a distinction can be made between the day-to-day routine in schools and classrooms, on the one hand, and attempts to study that routine and to suggest ways in which it might be improved, on the other; with a corresponding distinction between practising teachers and what, according to accepted usage, are called educational theorists. Practising teachers and educational theorists are both concerned, in their different ways, with the achievement of the same overall purpose, that of bringing about education. The educational theorists are therefore involved in the practice of teaching, even although they may not be involved in daily, face-to-face contacts with children or students. Rather than educational *theorists*, they are perhaps more accurately described as educational *practitioners*.[6]

This conclusion seems less paradoxical if it is remembered that most educational theorists are lecturers in colleges of education, where their primary job is the training of teachers. They are themselves teachers, indeed, teachers of teachers and therefore have an important part to play in the practice of teaching. Since a practice is carried on in accordance with the guidance provided by a tradition, teacher training will primarily take the form of introducing intending teachers to that tradition and thus making the guidance which it provides available to them. The tradition concerned not only allows but also encourages and even requires constant criticism and change. In terms of the distinction made in the previous chapter, it is a critical and not a conservative tradition. Provision must therefore be made not only to allow intending teachers to become acquainted with the guidance which tradition provides, so that they become aware of the currently accepted practice, but also to make it possible for them to evaluate and criticise that practice. An education lecturer, in being a teacher of teachers, therefore has an additional reason for engaging in the evaluation and criticism of the practice of teaching.

Thus although evaluation and criticism are an integral part of teaching in a critical tradition, they are bound to be of secondary importance where practising teachers are concerned, while there is reason to expect them to be given greater priority by those engaged in teacher training. Indeed there is no reason why, within the total practice of teaching, some individuals should not specialise wholly in critical appraisal. The main point is that, provided they are primarily concerned with suggesting ways in which the practice of teaching might be improved rather than motivated only by intellectual curiosity, they are part of that practice rather than external to it. In this way what is called educational theory is really part of educational practice. It nevertheless remains possible that the evaluation and criticism of teaching practice, and in due course of established practice, may be based to a greater or lesser extent on theoretical considerations; for example, on psychological discoveries about the nature of the learning process and the development of intelligence. That possibility must now be considered.

2. The technology of teaching

Anyone considering how the practice of teaching might be improved is bound to be influenced by the broader cultural tradition to which that practice belongs, which is a tradition that accords a place of central importance to science and its achievements. The suggestion that teaching should be placed on a scientific basis is therefore bound to be taken seriously; indeed, according to the *Concise Oxford Dictionary*, pedagogy *is* the science of teaching. It has been argued that teaching is a practice, the overall purpose of which, the bringing about of learning, is practical rather than theoretical; it is not a branch of enquiry, like physics, biology or psychology, the purpose of which is the discovery of truths, and therefore it cannot literally be a science. What presumably is meant is that pedagogy is concerned with the theoretical principles on which teaching should be based. It would be more accurate to define it as the technology rather than the science of teaching, since it is concerned with the application of scientific principles for a practical purpose.

It cannot be taken for granted that for every practice there is a related technology. Some practices clearly do have technologies, for example, building, farming and medicine, but even in these cases whereas the practices are very ancient the technology is very new. For example, people have been making use of various herbs in the treatment of the sick since ancient times without knowing why they have such healing properties. With the development of organic chemistry it has become possible to isolate and often to synthesise the active ingredient involved, and this, combined with increasing knowledge of the functioning of the body, has made it possible to discover why the herbs work in the way they do. Thus foxglove was used to treat heart disease, as described for example in George Eliot's *Silas Marner*, long before digitalis was extracted from it. In this and similar ways modern medicine has come to be based on the sciences of biology and chemistry and the treatment of disease has ceased to be the hit and miss affair it once was. This is not at present true of all diseases but there is reason to hope that at some time in the future it will be. Medicine thus provides an outstanding example of a practice which, although it now has an appropriate technology, did not always have one and makes the point that it should not be assumed that in all cases a practice *must* have its own technology.

The example of medicine suggests that those practices which do not at present have a supporting technology can nevertheless be expected to acquire one in the future, with the fact that they do not already have one being explained in one of two ways. First, the scientific principles which would make this possible have not yet been discovered. However, given our belief in science and scientific progress we suppose that there must be principles to be discovered and that they will in fact be discovered in due course. Secondly, even though the relevant scientific principles have been discovered, the practices concerned may fail to make adequate use of them; there is bound to be a considerable time lag before the relevance of scientific principles is appreciated and their application to practice worked out. Taking these factors into account it seems as though our belief in scientific progress obliges us to conclude that all practices either have or at some time in the future will have an appropriate technology.

There is still a further possibility. Because of the kind of practice they are, some practices may rest on knowledge and understanding of a kind to which scientific progress is irrelevant. In this case the reason they lack a technology is because there is no scope for developing one rather than because no progress has been made. It was suggested earlier that those engaged in the practice of teaching need to know both what to do and how to set about it. To know what to do in any practice is to be acquainted with its overall purpose, and that is not a matter of either actual or possible scientific knowledge. This is true even in the case of medicine; to know that the purpose of medicine is to heal the sick is to know something which neither is nor could be a piece of scientific knowledge. In no case, therefore, can a practice be identified with its technology. But the present suggestion goes further than this. It is that in some cases the knowledge of how to achieve the ends of practice also may lie outside the scope of science.

Religion provides a very clear example of this possibility. Like teaching or medicine, religion can be thought of as a social practice identified by its overall purpose and from the point of view of its practitioners that purpose must be religious. Exactly how it should be described is not important from the present point of view, but presumably some reference must be made to God. Let us suppose that the purpose of engaging in religious practices is to bring those who engage in them into a closer and more loving relation with God. Then the means to this end will be such things as communal worship, prayer and meditation, and it seems manifestly absurd to suppose that prayer, for example, could be made more effective in achieving that end by being placed on a scientific basis. Extensive use of technology may of course be made in more mundane ways, for example, to restore or heat church buildings, to get to church and so on, or even to test the historical authenticity of holy relics such as the Turin shroud; but all of this is peripheral to the main purpose of worship.

A distinction can therefore be made between those practices which are based on scientific principles and are in that sense sciences, and those which are not and which may therefore be called arts. Candidates for the arts in this sense include not only religion but also painting, literature and, of course, teaching. In so far as teaching is a science it can and presumably should be reduced to a routine for dealing with each situation in accordance with rules based on scientific principles; perhaps one day it may even be mechanised or computerised. In so far as it is an art it depends primarily on skill in dealing with people, based on knowledge and understanding of them as individuals. Teaching can still be done well or badly but success will depend primarily on the personality of the teacher. Hints and rules of thumb are possible but since the personality of the teacher is variable what works for one person may not do so for another.

Given the distinction between arts and sciences, the question which arises is whether teaching is a science or an art. What makes it difficult to suppose that religion could have its own technology, and in that sense constitute a science, is what makes it the kind of practice which it is, its overall purpose. I suggested earlier that however this is described in detail, it must include a central reference to God, and since God clearly lies outside the scope of science, it is difficult to see how the establishment of a relation with God could be based on scientific principles. I have already suggested that the overall purpose of teaching is the bringing about of education, and in a later chapter will argue that to become educated is to learn to be a person. Whether or not that is correct, it is at least obvious that education is essentially concerned with people *as* people, in contrast to orthodox medicine, which is primarily concerned with the functioning of their bodies. It is this connection between teaching and persons which makes it especially difficult to decide whether teaching is a science or an art.

Whether teaching is a science depends firstly on the possibility of a science of human behaviour and secondly on the extent to which that possibility has been realised. The most ambitious attempt to establish such a science is that of behaviouristic psychology, recently applied to teaching under the heading of behaviour modification. The behaviourist conception of man and human nature is essentially Lockean. The behaviour of a person at any moment of time is presented as a function of his situation at that time and of his behaviour at earlier times; and that, in turn, was a function of his situation at those times. Man is thus the product of his experiences and what he becomes can be controlled by controlling his experiences. Such a view of man can be contrasted with the emphasis placed by the Gombrich point of view on the importance of a person's social situation, including his participation in social practices such as painting and teaching. The relation between a person's social situation and that person's behaviour in that situation is not one of cause and effect. The person's behaviour depends not on his situation as such, but on his perception of it. And that perception does not cause him to behave as he does, but merely suggests to him the appropriateness of doing so. Acceptance of such a view therefore makes it difficult to see what scope there could be for a science of human behaviour.

Whether teaching is an art or a science has implications for the training of teachers. At the beginning of this section I suggested that those engaged in a social practice such as teaching need to know both what to do and how to do it, and that they are guided in answering these questions by the tradition in accordance with which the practice is carried out. Whether teaching is an art or a science, therefore, teacher training will still primarily take the form of introducing intending teachers to that tradition. The most important thing which they will get from it is a sense of overall purpose; that is, some idea of what they are up to. Only after they have a clear idea of what they are doing will they be in a position to consider how to do it. Given that, however, the view that teaching is a science suggests the need for a college-based training to allow the relevant technology to be acquired and the scientific principles on which it is based to be understood. This can best be done with the help of lecturers who are specialists in the branches of enquiry to which those principles belong and who are also familiar with the actual practice of teaching. The view that teaching is a science therefore provides a rationale for the existence of specialised teacher-training colleges or, as they are now called, colleges of education. The view that teaching is an art suggests the need for the teacher to learn the job under the guidance of a more experienced colleague, on the lines of a master-craftsman and his apprentice. In fact, of course, teacher training reflects both views by combining college-based lectures of a more theoretical kind with teaching practice in local schools.

3. *The curriculum*

The idea of a curriculum is closely connected with the ideas of teaching and learning. In discussing the teacher-pupil model of teaching in Chapter 1, it was pointed out that teaching is one of the sorts of things which people do. It is a kind of action and depends on its intention for being the kind of action which it is. The standard intention involved in teaching is that of helping someone to learn. Learning will be considered more fully later but two points must be made now. First, to have learnt something is, in a very broad sense, to have got something right; learning involves a kind of success. Secondly, if someone has learnt something, then it must be possible to say what he has learnt. In other words, learning must have some content, since to learn is necessarily to learn something. These two points are connected, since the success which occurs when learning takes place must be related to its content, and both have important consequences for teaching. Teaching is successful only if learning takes place, since to teach is to try to help someone to learn. Thus the success of the teacher depends on the success of the learner; the teacher will have succeeded only if the learner learns what the teacher intended him to learn. If the teacher is to have any chance of success – indeed, if anything is to count as success – he must know what he intends the learner to learn. Not only must learning have some content, it must have the content which the teacher intended it to have. One of the things which any teacher needs to know therefore is what to teach. Nothing is laid down by the teacher-pupil model of teaching, however, as to what the content of teaching should be or, indeed, as to who should decide what it is to be. From the point of view provided by the teacher-pupil model, it looks as though the teacher is free to decide for himself what to teach and, for that matter, who to teach and when, where and how to do so.

As far as it goes, this conclusion is perfectly acceptable; indeed, in this respect teaching is no different from many of the sorts of things which people do. For example, they buy things, go for little walks, have things for breakfast and so on; for the most part they are free to buy what they like, to decide when and where to go for their walk, and whether to have marmalade on their toast for breakfast and whether to dunk it in their tea or coffee. There are some things which are prohibited by law, such as murder and theft, but teaching is not one of them, and the law, in saying what cannot be done, implicitly defines an area of freedom within which people may do as they choose. But although the account of teaching given above is all right as far as it goes, it is clearly inadequate if what we are interested in is the activities of those who accept responsibility for bringing about learning in socially structured situations. To be a teacher in this sense is not simply to adopt a certain intention but to occupy a social role in a social institution of an appropriate kind, that is, in a teaching institution such as a school, college or university. From this point of view a school is simply a set of relatively stable arrangements for regulating the activities of teachers, including their relations with each other and with those they teach.

Such arrangements will depend on some idea, however vaguely formulated, of what the overall purpose of the school is, about what the school is *for*. That purpose may be defined narrowly as, for example, to teach people to drive, or it may be defined very broadly as the provision of an education for those who attend it. It is of course schools of the latter kind which are primarily of interest here but in either case something must be decided about what is to be taught, and if that decision is to make any claim to rationality it must bear some intelligible relation to the overall purpose of the school. And the school itself must fit into the overall pattern of the school system of a city or county and of the country as a whole.

Whatever is taught in a school (or other educational institution), must be intended to make some contribution to the education of those who attend it. As clear a view as possible of what it is to be educated is therefore essential. In a later chapter I will suggest that to become educated is to learn to become a person. In doing so, however, my intention will be to give an account of what makes *any* tradition recognisable as an educational tradition, including traditions which are very different from our own, resting as they do on different conceptions of what a person should be. What is needed to give sense and direction to decisions about what is to be taught, therefore, is an understanding of what counts as being educated according to the particular educational tradition concerned. Attempts to articulate such an understanding are made by philosophies of education of the kind discussed at the beginning of this chapter.

However, the guidance provided by a philosophy of education is also bound to be very general. For example, it may suggest that account be taken of the age and ability of the child without saying precisely how they should be taken into account. A school, however, must make more detailed plans about the content of the teaching which takes place in it. As argued at the beginning of this section, anything which can be learnt is, *prima facie*, a candidate for that content. But to be acceptable it must be seen as contributing to the education of those being taught. A curriculum is an account of what is thought of as acceptable from that point of view. It is an elaboration and articulation of the content of education from the point of view of a particular philosophy of education.

The use of words like 'planning' and 'decision' may suggest that a curriculum must be formulated explicitly after having been consciously worked out and adopted at some time in the past, but this need not be the case. Just as a philosophy of education is better understood as an attempt to describe the pre-existing commitment embodied in a living tradition than as a premeditated ideology, so also a curriculum is primarily a description of existing practice. There are of course extended exercises in what are called curriculum planning or curriculum development, some of which may indeed present themselves as filling in a blank cheque of infinite possibility. But if they do this is misleading. In a critical tradition such as our own it is to be expected that all aspects of existing practice, including the content of teaching, should be subject to constant criticism and evaluation, and that these should lead to proposals for change. But there are limits to what can sensibly be suggested which are laid down not only by the educational tradition concerned but also, on the one hand, by the broader cultural tradition of which it is a part and, on the other, by the tradition of the particular school concerned. As Gombrich points out in the quotation from *Art and Illusion* at the beginning of the previous chapter, 'not everything is possible in every period'. Thus in the modern scientific age, science must have a place in any curriculum even if, in some schools, only by the side of the classics.

If explicit curriculum planning or development is thought necessary, then some decision must be made as to who is to do it. Broadly speaking, who that is to be will depend on whether the practice of teaching is organised as a profession or bureaucratically; if the former, then it will be the teachers themselves, if the latter, then it will be the government. In practice, of course, both will wish to be consulted, whichever has the major role, as also may others, for example parents and business and commercial organisations. It is likely, although not inevitable, that a government planning body will think primarily in terms of so-called national need and try to impose a uniform pattern over the whole country, whereas one set up by teachers is more likely to think in terms of the education and welfare of individuals and to show sensitivity to local traditions and needs. Acceptance of Lockean presuppositions, including an assumption of knowledge of *a priori* practical principles which are independent of existing practice, will make belief in the possibility and desirability of strong central planning, whether by teachers or government, more probable.

Finally, mention must be made of a syllabus, which provides a detailed statement of the contents of a part of the curriculum which is to be dealt with in a particular course. Syllabuses are important from the point of view of public examinations, since they allow candidates to know what they will be examined on and allow all candidates to be tested by the same questions, thus making comparisons between candidates from different schools and areas possible. From the planning point of view, however, they come last in order of importance. The first thing that must be decided is what the overall purpose of the school or school system is. That must then be given content through a curriculum. Only then can the immediate goals of particular courses, designed for children or students at a particular stage, be formulated. The formulation of precise goals without regard for any overall pattern simply because they offer a kind of objectivity is no more than a meaningless exercise.

CHAPTER 4 ACCOUNTABILITY

The following cautionary tale, being a brief account of the life of Joseph Lancaster, is offered by way of introduction to the topic of the present chapter. Joseph Lancaster was born in Southwark in 1778. His father's pension as an old soldier added to his earnings as a sieve-maker gave the family a position 'decent and comfortable but still not so far raised above the poor as to open the prospects of ambition'. His son Joseph, however, was of exceptional ability. He ran away at the age of fourteen to Jamaica to teach the negro slaves, returned home hoping to join the dissenting ministry, was prevented from doing so by becoming a Quaker, and became a teacher instead.

In 1798 he opened his first school, which was so successful and expanded so rapidly that he could not cope with all the pupils it attracted. Lacking the money to pay assistants, 'the idea occurred to him of making the boys who knew a little teach the boys who knew less, and he thought he had made one of the most useful discoveries in the history of civilisation' – and was confirmed in this opinion after obtaining the patronage of George III. Success, however, apparently went to his head. 'His recklessness, his extravagance, and his ostentation almost pass belief.'

Debt followed, and after six months in the King's Bench Prison a Society was formed by Joseph Lancaster, William Corston and Joseph Fox to promote the education of the poor – in effect, to back Lancaster and look after his affairs, still in a financial mess. This was not wholly successful, however. 'The Committee realised that the money it collected was given to it for the promotion of education; Lancaster thought that it was given to him for his own use – that the Committee had the privilege of increasing his income but not the right of regulating his expenditure.' After unsuccessfully trying to start a rival to the original Borough Road school, Lancaster broke with the

society in 1813, 'sank into complete obscurity and deep
poverty', left England for the New World in 1818, and 'finished
joy and moan' in New York in 1838. (Based on the introduction
to David Salmon's edition of Lancaster's *Improvements in Education*, Cambridge University Press, 1932. All quotations are taken
from Salmon's introduction.)

I. ACTIONS AND ACCOUNTABILITY

In the previous chapter I pointed out that people may be said to
be the authors or agents of their actions in the sense that their
actions originate with them and therefore that they may be said
to be responsible for the changes which they bring about or
cause by their actions. It is only because people are responsible
in this basic agency sense that it makes sense to hold them
socially responsible or accountable and therefore to praise or
blame and reward or punish them for what they do. In this
chapter the idea of accountability will be examined in some
detail but first I will say a little more about actions in order to
prepare the background and to try to explain why it is thought
appropriate to regard people as accountable for what they do.

First, in what has already been said it has been taken for
granted that actions are always attributable *to someone*, that is, to
the person or agent with whom the action orginates. Thus in
relation to any action, for example the killing of Cock Robin, it
will always make sense to ask who did it. Unless we know who
did it (that is, who was causally responsible for Cock Robin's
death) we will not know who to hold socially responsible or
accountable for it, since the person held responsible must be the
same person as the person who did it. Secondly, in acting
persons are aware of the situation in which they are acting and
of the change which they intend to bring about by their action.
In order to be actions in the relevant sense, they must be guided
by beliefs and directed by intentions. For example, I cannot be
said to feed the cat unless I believe that there is a cat to be fed
and I intend, in doing what I do, to bring it about that the cat is
fed. Thirdly, the person must adopt some method or means of
changing things in the way intended and he must believe that by
doing what he does things will in fact be changed in that way.

For example, in order to feed the cat I may put some Al Cat Munchies in his bowl, having at least some expectation that he will eat them. Finally, the change which it is intended to bring about may not in fact be brought about; putting it another way, people do not always achieve the goals which they set themselves. The cat may not be hungry or, if hungry, may be unwilling to eat the food which is offered.

Actions in this sense, which involve beliefs and intentions, may be contrasted not only with the action of inanimate forces of nature, such as that of waves on the base of a cliff, but also with the behaviour of simple animals which seems to be no more than an unthinking, automatic response, either innate or learnt, to stimuli currently presented by their environment. Many people think that at least some animals other than man do act in the sense indicated above. Whether such a view could be defended need not be considered in the present context. The point is that, even if it is admitted that cats, for example, do act in the above sense it does not follow that it would be thought appropriate to hold them socially responsible or accountable for what they do. We may well think that the cat killed the canary without also thinking that it would make sense to blame or punish it for doing so, although we might try to train it not to kill birds in future or to stop it from doing so by hanging a bell around its neck.

This suggests the need for a further distinction between actions in the minimal sense indicated above and actions in a fuller sense which allows us to see why a person is regarded as responsible for what he does whereas a cat is not. It has been suggested that a cat may be an agent in the sense that its behaviour is guided by beliefs and directed by intentions and therefore that it is aware of the situation in which it is acting and of the change which it intends to bring about through acting. Persons, however, are aware not simply of their situation and their effect on it but also of themselves as in and acting on that situation. They not only *are* agents but are aware of themselves *as* agents, since they not only do things but also know that they are doing them and what they are doing. Their actions are attributable to them not only by others, as when we say that the cat killed the canary, but also by themselves; they see their actions as *their* actions and would accordingly use the first person pronoun in any description of them. Thus persons possess not only awareness but self-awareness. And they are aware, also, that other people are aware that this is so.

The position of a person who is aware of his beliefs and intentions is very different from that of a cat which simply has beliefs and intentions. To have a belief of any kind is to discriminate amongst perceived possibilities. For example, it is to see the cat's being on the mat as one possibility among others. It is therefore possible for a person to believe that the cat is on the mat only if it is also possible for them to suppose that the cat might not have been on the mat. Indeed we would not describe a creature as having beliefs unless it were prepared to change its beliefs in the light of changing circumstances; for example, to change the belief that the cat is on the mat to the belief that the cat is not on the mat when the cat moves from the mat. If our beliefs did not discriminate amongst possibilities in this way they could not provide us with information about the world. To be aware of a belief is in effect to believe that you have that belief; it is therefore to realise that your belief might be different from what it is. And it is this realisation – of the possibility of an alternative – which makes it possible for a person to reflect on his beliefs and hold them up for critical examination. Similarly, to have an intention is to intend to change things in ways which are foreseen so that they are this way rather than that; for example it is to intend to put the cat out for the night rather than to leave it in the kitchen. To realise that you have an intention is not only to have that intention but also to realise that you might have had a different intention. It is therefore to be in a position to look critically at the intentions which you do have. Thus a person who is aware of himself as an agent is able to suppose that he might have acted differently, whereas the cat that killed the canary was not.

In order to be held responsible for what he does, however, a person must not only be able to *suppose* that he might have acted differently but must also be able to *act* differently. When a person is described as acting differently, for example as going to bingo instead of staying home with the children, or vice versa, reference is made to two actions, one of which he did (in this case, go to bingo) and the other of which he did not do (in this case, stay at home). The ability to act differently in the required sense consists therefore of two further abilities. The person concerned must be able to do what he actually does do and he must also be able not-to-do what he does not do. The first of these is relatively straightforward – if a person does something then he must be able to do it – but the second, which is not simply the negation of the first, is not. To say that a person can not-drink, for example, is to take for granted rather than to deny that he can drink. It is to say something quite different, that he can refrain from drinking and, therefore, that he is in a position to choose whether to drink. We normally suppose that people are free agents in the sense that their actions are the result of choice and that the position of an alcoholic, who cannot give up drink, even although he knows what it would be like to do so, is exceptional. But we also in effect suppose that what is exceptional for human beings is always the case, and in that sense natural, for cats. That is why a person is normally regarded as responsible for what he does whereas a cat is not. We do not blame the cat for killing the canary because that is what cats are like, meaning by this not simply that cats are disposed to kill canaries but that they have no control over what they do and cannot, therefore, be said to choose to do it.

To summarise, it is thought appropriate to hold persons responsible for what they do (i) because, in being aware of themselves as agents, they are able to suppose that they might have acted differently and (ii) because, at least in most cases, they would in fact have been able to act differently. Nothing has been said so far, however, about why it should be a matter of concern whether persons act or refrain from acting in certain ways and why they should be liable to be criticised for doing so. What a person does can be criticised, firstly, as not in that person's real or long-term interest and therefore as imprudent. Criticism of this sort depends on a view of what that person's real or long-term interest consists in. For example, it is now widely recognised that, as the government health warning puts it, smoking can seriously damage your health. Secondly, actions can be criticised by reference to impersonal standards of one kind or another which require persons to behave or refrain from behaving in certain ways. Such standards are provided by explicitly formulated legal rules backed by the authority and coercive power of the state and by moral rules which, although

they do not have that backing, may have even greater authority.
Legal and moral rules are a formalisation of the most general
aspects of the social framework provided by the way of seeing
and doing of a community. It was argued in the previous
chapter that the various social activities, such as education or
medicine, which form part of the total life of a community have
their own ways of seeing and doing and conduct themselves
according to their own traditions. This provides a point of view
from which the conduct of those engaged in them can be assessed
which is additional to the more general way of seeing and doing
of the community as a whole.

What people do is, therefore, a matter of concern both to
themselves and others, because they see themselves as engaged
in social activities and, more generally, as sharing a way of life,
with others; they see others, and others as seeing them, in the
same way. They see themselves and others, therefore, as
constrained by the standards which those activities and that
way of life impose.

II. ACCOUNTS

Teaching, as pointed out in Chapter 1, is one of the sorts of
things which people do and therefore for which they may be
held accountable. It is perhaps worth remembering also that, in
the context of philosophy of education, it is the activities of
teachers who are part of a social practice of teaching which are
primarily of interest.

1. *Accounts as stories*
To be accountable is to be required, or to be liable to be
required, to give an account of what you have done or omitted
to do, and to give an account is, first and foremost, to *say* what
you have done.

Financial accounts, of the kind produced by accountants,
illustrate this very clearly. Public companies produce annual
accounts in accordance with their memoranda and articles of
association and the requirements of the Companies Acts. The
accounts themselves are produced by professionally qualified
accountants from records kept for the purpose by the company

itself; what they provide is a summary, in financial terms, of what has happened during the period of time, normally one year, to which they relate. They summarise the financial transactions in which the company has been engaged during the year, setting out expenses and receipts and resultant profit or loss in a profit and loss account and recording changes in assets and liabilities in a balance sheet.

Of course, not all accounts are financial; indeed, financial accounts are highly specialised and in many respects not typical. For example, the detective may ask you to give an account of your movements on such and such a date. The barman may be asked by the club secretary to account for the missing bottles of whisky, and so on. But in all cases to give an account is simply to tell a story about what happened on a particular occasion or during a particular period of time.

2. *Accounts as histories*

Financial accounts are produced at the end of the financial year, when all of the information relating to that year is available. They are therefore after-the-event or *ex post* accounts. In presenting them to the shareholders at the annual general meeting, the directors are giving an account of what they have done. Accounts are thus produced too late to influence the course of the events to which they relate. The information contained in them may provide a basis for planning for the future, in which case they may indirectly influence future events. But the accounts themselves are *histories* in the sense that they tell us what *has* happened. It might be argued that the ordinary usage of the word 'account' does not support the view that accounts relate exclusively to the past. But even if this were so, it would still be important to make the contrast between accounts of past events and expressions of plans or intentions for the future, and it is the former which are relevant to the idea of accountability. Correspondingly, a history is an attempt to give an account of and provide a point of view from which to make sense of an individual's or a group's past.

3. *Personal involvement in accounts*

Accounts are stories about what has happened in the past; they are histories. Not all histories, however, are accounts in the relevant sense. Only first person accounts, singular or plural, which make use of the words 'I' or 'we', are relevant to the issue of accountability. For example, 'I was picking roses when . . .', 'we were driving home when . . .', 'I was just looking at it when . . .', and so on. Accounts prepared by a third party such as an accountant are usually presented in an impersonal form but are first person accounts none the less since they are prepared at the request of and on behalf of the company concerned, not simply out of intellectual curiosity. Furthermore, the person telling the story must have been actively involved in the events which he describes, unlike the narrator in a novel who sees everything that happens but takes no part in the action. And the story which is told must make the teller's own part clear in the events which are being described. In particular, an account will be expected of what he did, either in person or through an agent authorised to act on his behalf. What he did, in this context, means what he was, or is presumed to have been, responsible for as agent.

Accounts of the relevant kind are first person accounts and they are accounts of what that person did rather than of events which he simply witnessed. However, it is important to notice that it is not always easy to decide what a person is responsible for in the agency sense. We could not be held responsible for running over the pig, for example, unless the pig was run over; but it does not follow that we were responsible for its being run over even if we were driving the car that hit it. It is unlikely that we intended to hit it and, indeed, presumably made every effort to avoid doing so. In that sense, the pig's being run over was clearly an accident. But we were driving the car which ran over the pig, so that although we did not intend to run over it, the pig's being run over was a direct consequence of something which we did. Also, it might be suggested, the pig would not have been run over had we been driving with more care. More generally, persons may be required to provide an account not only of their actions (in the sense indicated in section II) but also of the consequences of their actions, whether those consequences were intended or not. As consequences become increasingly remote and indirect, and hence unforeseeable, and as other factors intervene, it becomes increasingly unreasonable to regard persons as accountable for them. In general, a person is liable to be asked for an account of what was, or what should have been, under his control, but no firm line can be drawn independently of particular cases. What seems reasonable, indeed, will for the most part be laid down by the tradition concerned.

4. *Concerning yourself with and being concerned about what others do*

So far accounts have been considered from the point of view of those who are required to provide them. I want now to look at them from the opposite point of view, that is from the point of view of those who ask for or require them and, therefore, for whom the account is provided. In this connection I would like to make a distinction between *concerning yourself with* what others do, in the sense of taking an interest in and wanting to know about it, on the one hand, and *being concerned about* what others do, in the sense of caring about and perhaps being involved in some way in what they do.

(a) Concerning yourself with what others do

It is natural for people to be interested in and curious about what is happening around them, especially about other people and what they are up to. Human life would be very different if this were not so. Nevertheless, at least in our society, people are thought to have a right to privacy in what might be called their private lives: for example, about their financial affairs, health, sexual life, religious beliefs and generally what goes on in the privacy of their own homes. Other people have a reason, therefore, not to concern themselves with these matters, and if they do so their concern may be labelled *improper*. People also take an interest in what others do even when their interest is not improper in this way even though they have no reason to do so other than curiosity. Such interest may be friendly or neighbourly rather than mischievous or malicious and is not in itself objectionable, although there is no obligation on those who excite it to satisfy such curiosity. Concern which is neutral in this way may be called *simple* concern. Where the line is drawn between simple and improper concern is largely a matter of local convention and may become blurred or extended in the case of those, such as royalty or entertainers, whose function or job invites public interest.

(b) Being concerned about what others do

People also concern themselves with what others do because
they are concerned about them and about what they do. Such
concern may arise directly because they care about these people
and what happens to them, looking on them as friends, lovers,
parents or simply as fellow human beings. Concern may also
arise out of the more structured situations considered in the
previous chapter, such as that between teacher and pupil or
doctor and patient. In such cases concern will be limited, at least
in the first instance, to the special aspect of the interest of others
to which their attention is directed by their professional
purpose. Teachers, for example, are concerned about the
education of their pupils, and so will be concerned about
whether they pay attention in class, do well in exams and about
their educational progress in general. Similarly doctors will be
concerned about whether their patients follow prescribed
courses of treatment, eat sensibly, smoke or drink to excess, and
about their health generally.

Secondly, people may be concerned about what others do
either because their own interests or the interests of those they
care about are affected, or because the interests of those they
have a duty to look after are affected. For example, parents are
interested in what teachers do because what teachers do affects
their children and they care what happens to their children.
Conversely, teachers are interested in how parents treat their
children (whether, for example, they allow young children to
stay up very late) because they care about the children's
educational progress and that may be affected by home
circumstances.

In all these cases, people have a reason for being concerned
with what others do which is likely to be accepted as a good
reason for concerning themselves with the actions of others, both
by those in whose activities they interest themselves and by third
parties. They may therefore be said to be properly concerned or
to have a *proper concern* about what others do. Anyone who has
such a concern will think it reasonable to ask for an account of
what others are doing, perhaps as a matter of routine and
certainly if they think things are not going well. Recognition of
the reasonableness of that request can similarly be expected to
lead to a willingness to provide an account. There may also be
reasons for not doing so. For example, a doctor may refuse to

discuss a patient's health with anyone else, however legitimate their concern, on the grounds that this would be a violation of confidentiality, and for similar reasons a teacher may refuse to discuss one student's exam results with another. On the other hand, concerned others may be in a position to require a person to give an account of his activities or actions. For example, the stockholders of a public company are entitled to receive audited accounts of the company's activities, and the police and courts are empowered to demand an account from those involved, directly or indirectly, in suspected wrongdoing.

Finally, there are some things with which people not only may properly concern themselves but with which they ought to concern themselves. The story of the Good Samaritan draws attention to the concern which any person should have about the fate of other human beings. In some cases, therefore, concern may not simply be proper but *required*. Once again, there may be disagreement about what people are required to be concerned about: obvious examples which suggest themselves are the chronically sick, third world poverty and the victims of famine and prolonged brutal war. Even although there does not seem to be much which most of us can do about such things, they are matters which we ought to care about and, although there might be disagreement about this also, which we have a duty to inform ourselves about.

5. Reactions to accounts

Accounts, it can now be suggested, originate in the proper concern of one person, who will be referred to as the second party, about what someone else, the first party, has done. The primary function of an account is therefore to provide the second party with information about the activities of the first. Since the desire for information is based on proper concern rather than idle curiosity, some reaction to it is to be expected. Moreover, the events which form the subject matter of the account are, or are presumed to be, under the control of the first party. Reactions to an account, based on concern about those events, are therefore likely to take the form of questions such as: 'Why did you do this, rather than that or the other, which you very well might have done had you chosen to do so?'; or 'Would it not have been better had you done this or that, rather than what you did?'; or even 'You have (or have not) done well'. If things have clearly not been going well, it may seem appropriate to ask what steps are being taken to ensure that they go better in future. For example, schools are now required to publish GCE examination results, and if the results are obviously disappointing parents may well wish to know what steps are being taken to make sure that they are better in future.

In providing information in this way accounts put others in a position to evaluate and assess and perhaps also to criticise or commend what has been done. It follows, of course, that an excellent way of avoiding criticism, or at least informed criticism, is by refusing to supply the information on which it might be based. Totalitarian governments standardly impose a strict censorship on all forms of dissemination of information which might be politically sensitive, that is, might attract unfavourable attention. In fact all governments do this to a greater or lesser extent. Given that information is to be provided, those providing it may anticipate criticism and try to defend themselves from it in the accounts which they offer. In order to do so they are likely not just to describe what they have done but also to explain why they did it. Explanations of human actions differ in kind from explanations in science, where events are explained by subsuming them under covering laws and drawing attention to antecedent causes. Explanations of actions redescribe what was done in more general terms, making clear the part which that particular action played in the agent's life or in some more broadly defined activity in which the agent was engaged. For example, a company may explain in footnotes to its accounts that it closed a certain branch of the business because it had become unprofitable, or because the premises were needed for some other purpose. A school may explain that it no longer proposes to offer classical languages because there is little demand for them and they are no longer required for university entrance. Such explanations also function as justifications for what was done from the point of view of anyone who accepts the overall purpose of the activity assumed. Companies are in business to make profits and to point out that a course of action will increase profits is to provide a justification for taking it. The overall purpose of a school is less easily stated and may be the subject of considerable disagreement; nevertheless, for anyone who accepts university entrance as a major goal reference to it will function as a justification for changes in the subjects offered by the school.

It was pointed out earlier that persons do not always achieve what they set out to achieve and that their actions may have consequences which, although they may have been anticipated, were not intended. A company may make a loss rather than a profit, for example, or a school may have little success in getting students through O and A levels but acquire a reputation for behaviour problems instead. An attempt may therefore be made to anticipate the adverse comment which can be expected by pointing out that the assumption that things were under the control of the company or school was not wholly correct. The company's profitability may have been affected by changes in the cost of raw materials; for example, changes in the price of crude oil may have dramatic effects on oil company profits. Similarly, the school may explain its poor examination results and behaviour problem by pointing out that the more able children are 'creamed off' and that social conditions in its catchment area are bad. The ability to bring about change through human action is always subject to constraints of this sort imposed by an indifferent world which, even if they are anticipated, must be accommodated and cannot themselves be changed. It is therefore entirely appropriate for a person offering an account to draw attention to the constraints within which he was acting, thus explaining why his efforts took the form which they did or why they were less successful than had been hoped. For example, a remedial school may have a policy of accepting only those children which it thinks it can help, that is, those whose educational backwardness is remediable through the help the school can provide. This may mean that it is forced to refuse to accept children whose backwardness is due to circumstances beyond the school's control, such as emotional probems originating in the home, low intelligence and so on. This may seem harsh – the very opposite of an apparently more generous 'open doors' policy – but becomes intelligible once it is explained.

6. *The parties to an account*

(a) Some minor complications

The two parties directly involved in the presentation of an account are obviously the person providing the account and the

person for whom the account is intended, who have been
labelled the first and second parties, respectively. In practice the
position may be more complicated than this. First, as already
noted, the person actually providing the account may be doing
so on behalf of someone else on the basis of information supplied
by the first party. For example, the drawing up of a company's
accounts is a complex business which is undertaken only by a
professionally qualified accountant appointed for the purpose.
Secondly, the concern of the person for whom the account is
prepared may relate to a third party. For example, the teachers
in a school may be accountable to the governors, managers or
parents' committee who, in turn, are concerned about the pupils
of the school. Thirdly, although the *idea* of an account involves
that of two parties, the two parties may in fact be the same
person, while still allowing an account to fulfil its primary
purpose of providing information and making criticism and
assessment possible. A profession, for example, might be expected to want to monitor its own activities to see how far its
professional purposes are being achieved even if, in being
autonomous, it is not accountable to anyone else. Finally, the
first party (the party providing the account) may be either a
person, that is, a private individual such as John Smith or a
social entity such as a company or school, and this makes a
difference to their accountability. The position of each will
therefore be considered below.

(b) Persons as accountable

Any individual who is a person is liable to be asked to give an
account of his actions. However, he is normally asked to do so
only when there is reason to suppose that he has done something
wrong or discreditable so that, if it is established that he has in
fact done so, he becomes liable for punishment or blame. What
counts as doing wrong is defined by impersonal standards of one
kind or another, especially by moral and legal rules which
formalise the more central aspects of ways of doing laid down by
traditions. The individual thus becomes accountable, in the
sense of being required to give an account of himself, only when
he has, *prima facie*, done something wrong as defined in this way.
Conversely, when there has been no *prima facie* wrong done, he
may still be *able* but cannot be *required* to give an account of his

activities. And in giving an account of himself he may deny that he has done what he is said to have done (in effect, he may plead not guilty) or, as suggested earlier, he may try to present what he has done in a different light ('I wasn't stealing it, I was just borrowing it', for example).

It is this situation, concerned with the moral or legal responsibility of the individual person, which has received most attention in philosophy. It was argued in Chapter 1, however, that philosophy of education should concern itself with teaching as a social activity and is therefore primarily concerned with teachers only as practitioners in a teaching practice in which they occupy well-defined social roles in social institutions such as schools and colleges. It will be argued in the rest of this subsection that social entities such as social institutions and the occupants of social roles are individuals of a different sort from persons and that this makes a difference in deciding for what they can sensibly be held to be accountable.

(c) Social entities as accountable

According to the Lockean view outlined in Chapter 2, man is a rational individualist who may enter into social relations with other men in order to achieve pre-existing desires more efficiently but does not thereby bring into existence a social entity or individual of a wholly new kind. We talk, on this view, as though there were such things as communities and social institutions but this is no more than a convenient way of talking and does not commit us to supposing that there really are such things. This view was clearly expressed by Jeremy Bentham, who remarked in his 'Introduction to the Principles of Morals and Legislation' that 'the community is a fictitious body, composed of the individual persons who are considered as it were its members'.[1] If this view were correct then strictly speaking there would not be any individuals other than persons who could be held accountable for what they do.

Even if this view is accepted, it has to be admitted that we do not always speak strictly and that in our social and legal practices we speak as though there were entities other than persons who might be held responsible for what they do. The clearest example is that of a legal person, for example a public company or local authority, which is treated by the law as though it were a person for legal purposes. Of course, a company can act only through its officials but when an official enters into a contract or borrows money on behalf of the company it is the company which has entered into the contract or borrowed the money, not the person who signs the relevant documents. A company then is an example of an entity which is recognised by the law as accountable (that is, legally accountable) for its actions even although it is not itself a person and indeed is dependent on the persons who are its officials to act on its behalf.

Bentham was well aware of the law's recognition of legal persons and regarded them, along with obligations and duties, as no more than fictitious entities like the community. On his view, we speak of them as existing for convenience of discourse but do not suppose that they really exist, in the way in which we suppose that persons exist. This preference for the individual rather than the community to which he belongs was rejected, however, by what was called the Gombrich view developed in Chapter 2, which stressed rather the interdependence of man and society. It is of course true that a society could not exist unless the persons who are its members exist but it is equally true that those persons could not be persons of the kind they are unless they were members of that society. Both exist in their own kind of way and each is dependent on the other for its existence. There are therefore entities other than persons – social entities – which might be held accountable, and these include educational institutions such as schools, colleges and universities.

It is obvious, however, that the way in which social entities such as companies, local authorities and schools exist is very different to that of persons. They are brought into existence – in the case of companies and local authorities by an explicit legal process – for a specific purpose, for example, to manufacture motor cars or to provide a fire or educational service. Persons, on the other hand, are born and in that sense occur naturally; they *have* purposes but, unlike artifacts and social institutions, are not, as such, there *for* a purpose. The legal process which brings social entities into existence (where there is a legal process) also confers powers on them, making it possible for them to achieve the purpose for which they were created. A local authority, for example, may be required to make educational provision for the children living within its area. In order to make this possible, it is given the right to raise money by local taxation and to use it to employ teachers and maintain buildings for them to teach in, thus bringing schools into existence.

Social entities such as schools are thus brought into being for a purpose and so have specific purposes built into them in a way in which persons do not. In this respect they are like artifacts, that is, things made for a purpose; a knife, for example, is something made to cut with. Persons on the other hand have purposes but are not there for a purpose. (This is not true for persons as the occupants of roles, for example, teachers in schools. Roles will be considered further in a later chapter.) This difference between social entities and persons makes a difference, as suggested earlier, to what they can sensibly be held accountable for. In general, the position so far as persons is concerned is that they are free to pursue their purposes, whatever they may happen to be, provided they are not prohibited from doing so by legal or other conventional rules. The advantage of being subject to the rule of law in this way is that it creates an area of freedom, allowing the individual to do whatever he wants to do provided the law does not forbid it. Persons are thus left to live their own lives within the limits laid down by the law and, in a less clearly defined way, by moral and other social conventions. They can be required to give an account of themselves only when they have *prima facie* gone beyond those limits; in other words, when they have done something wrong. A social entity such as a company or school, on the other hand, having been created for a purpose, may be asked to provide an account of its activities in order to allow those concerned to find out whether that purpose has in fact been achieved. Company accounts illustrate this very well; if a company was brought into being in order to make a profit out of manufacturing cars its shareholders can be expected to be concerned about how far it has succeeded in doing so. It is no doubt a simplification to say that all that matters is the profitability of a company; it may have other aims as well, such as long-term growth and stability, the creation of employment and so on. Even so, the purpose of a company is likely to be less contentious than that of a school, since there may well be disagreement about what is involved in providing education. However, despite this possibility of disagreement the fact remains that schools are brought into being for a purpose and that everybody knows, at least in general, what that purpose is.

To summarise, persons may be required to give an account of themselves only when there is reason to suppose that they have acted incorrectly in some way. Social entities such as schools and companies, on the other hand, may be required to show that they have done what they are supposed to have done. In this respect a social entity is like an artifact such as a vacuum cleaner. It is no defence of a vacuum cleaner to say that it never did anyone any harm; it can only be defended by showing that it has done some good by fulfilling the purpose for which it was manufactured, that of sucking up dust. The result is that whereas the question of an individual's being asked to give an account of himself arises only in exceptional circumstances, accountability may be a normal feature of the situation so far as social entities are concerned.

7. *Accounts and their contents*

(a) The production of accounts

The provision of an account is a human activity like any other; accordingly the form which it takes should reflect the purpose for which it is undertaken. That purpose is the provision of information about other activities and events in which the person providing the account was directly involved, thus allowing those for whom the account is provided to evaluate and assess what has been done. An account should therefore be sufficiently clear and accurate to make this possible.

In view of the fact that the accounts concerned are first person accounts, it might be thought that their provision would present no difficulty. According to the Lockean view developed in Chapter 2, a person is directly acquainted with his own ideas and therefore cannot but know what they are, whereas he cannot be acquainted with anyone else's ideas and can at best find out about them only indirectly. This feature of ideas has been extended to other mental phenomena, including the beliefs and intentions which give actions their character. It is supposed that an agent is directly acquainted with his own beliefs and intentions and consequently cannot but know what he is doing.

To take a simple example, if I am picking roses then I can be expected to know that I am, and if I know that I am then of course I am in a position to say that I am. Providing an account of what I am doing is therefore a straightforward matter.

However, providing an account is not as simple as this suggests. Firstly, other aspects of the Lockean account having been examined on their merits, there is no reason to retain this one unless it has independent support. In section I, a distinction was made between doing something and knowing what you are doing, the point being that you cannot reflect on what you are doing unless you are aware that you are doing it. A cat, it was suggested, is never aware of what it is doing, whereas a person may be and often is. And a person can be held responsible for what he does only because he is or can become aware of it, so that it is possible for him to reflect on his actions. Our concept of responsibility therefore depends on the fact that people are or are capable of becoming aware of what they are doing. This provides some support for the Lockean view and a similar insight lies behind Descartes' famous *cogito* argument. It does not follow, however, that people always know what they are doing simply because they are doing it, and if the facts are consulted it soon becomes obvious that in some cases, at least, they do not. Moreover, even if they know at the time, they tend to forget very quickly. (Did I set the proper number of essays last term? I cannot remember.)

Secondly, the claim being considered is that a person knows directly only what he himself is doing; indeed, knowledge of what other people are doing is admitted to be problematic and, at best, indirect. (In relation to Descartes' analogous view, it is this which gives rise to the so-called problem of other minds.) Therefore even if it is admitted it does not follow that when people are engaged in a co-operative enterprise with others, so that the word 'I' is replaced by the word 'we' in any account which they offer, that they will know, directly and infallibly, what they were collectively engaged in doing. Unless special channels of communication are developed, there is no reason why one person should know what the rest are doing. Moreover, a year in the life of a social entity such as a school is more than a catalogue of what the individual teachers in it have done during that year.

It would be a mistake to suppose that the drawing up of an account of a social entity is a straghtforward matter. Financial results of companies are in some ways the most straightforward type of account to produce. First, they are presented in monetary and therefore quantifiable terms. Secondly, the activity to which they relate has a well-defined standard purpose, the making of a profit, and this provides a principle of selection from the total mass of information potentially available. Finally, the motives of individuals are not normally in question, so that the problem of finding out what they are does not arise. Nevertheless the production of financial accounts is a matter of considerable difficulty and is normally undertaken only by those with the appropriate professional training. The production of an accurate, objective account of a school, by contrast, is intrinsically more difficult. First, it cannot be presented simply in monetary terms. (Of course, if a school is run as a business then financial accounts will be produced but that is another matter.) Public examination results are in themselves objective but provide little indication of how well the school itself is performing unless related to a variety of other factors, including the original academic potential of the students concerned. An attempt could be made to measure the latter by the use of intelligence tests; their use for selection purposes is no longer favoured but that again is another matter. There is no obvious way of quantifying other factors which affect academic performance, such as temperament, chronic illness and home background. Secondly, although I have suggested that schools do have a standard, built-in purpose, it is clearly not well-defined in the same way as commercial profit. The purpose of a school is to help its students to become educated, but there is room for considerable disagreement about what counts as becoming educated. Presumably most people would not wish to equate it in any straightforward way with passing exams.

(b) The content of an account

Finally, although closely connected with the topics discussed above, there is the question of what content an account should have. In general terms this question has already been answered. An account is primarily a description of what a person or social entity such as a school has done during a stated period of time, thus making evaluation and criticism possible. It is appropriate to ask persons to give an account of themselves only when they have at least *prima facie* done something wrong. In the case of a social entity such as a school which is brought into existence for a specific purpose, however, I have suggested that the point of an account is to put those concerned in a position to satisfy themselves that things are going as they should. The content of an account should therefore be determined by the purpose of the activity to which it relates.

Views about the content which an account of a school should have will therefore depend on some prior conception of what teachers are supposed to be doing in the first place. The main distinction here, which has already been anticipated, is between those who think of the teacher's job primarily in terms of education and those who see it in some more circumscribed way. Teachers themselves are more likely to think of the job in terms of education, especially if they constitute a profession as defined earlier, when it was suggested that professional teachers have a responsibility for determining the purpose of their own activity. It is possible also to see the teacher's job in a more limited way as, for example, preparing people for the work they will do in later life in manufacturing industry, commerce, the professions and so on. In that case the needs of industry are likely to be determined by industry, or perhaps by the government, rather than by teachers themselves.

Whatever view is taken of the purpose of teaching, a further question arises as to how far that purpose is being achieved. The more precisely that purpose is defined, the easier it will be to decide whether it has been achieved, but even if it is broadly defined in terms of education some criterion of educational attainment, such as examination performance, may have to be adopted.

8. *Responsibility and trust*

(a) Responsibility

Accounts, it has been suggested, are histories in the sense that they are produced *ex post facto*, that is, after the events to which they relate. They are therefore too late to influence those events. All they can do is provide information on the basis of which what has been done can be criticised and evaluated.

Accounts are not wholly without influence on the events to

which they relate. The knowledge that they will or may be required to give an account of themselves may well affect the way people conduct themselves. But the basic assumption is that those held accountable are responsible persons in the sense indicated in section II, 2(c) of Chapter 3 who can be be expected to do what they should to the best of their ability simply because they see that they should. Those seeing them in this way are assuming that they can be relied on, that is, trusted to do what they should without the need for anyone else to make sure that they do. In short, to hold people accountable for what they do is to treat them as responsible persons and therefore to trust them, since trust is the attitude appropriate to a responsible person. Supervision is not only unnecessary but also inappropriate, since it treats persons who are responsible as though they were not.

Perhaps the most central idea in the account of a profession given in Chapter 3 was that of responsibility for purpose. A member of a profession accepts responsibility not only for achieving but also for setting the overall purpose of his professional activities. It is this feature of a profession which leads naturally to public recognition and thence to autonomy. The members of a profession are not told by anyone else what to do and they are not subject to any external direction but it does not follow that no one else will be interested in what they do; on the contrary, it is to be expected and appropriate that others will be interested and that they should ask the profession to provide an account of its activities. Thus the idea of responsibility for purpose, as well as that of a responsible person, fits in well with that of accountability.

(b) Trust

I want now to turn to the other side of the picture. It is appropriate to ask for an account only from those regarded as responsible persons and perhaps also as responsible for purpose. To treat people as responsible in these ways is to trust them both to get things done and to decide what needs to be done. Trust is the counterpart of responsibility, and both are equally necessary if either is to play a part in social life or personal relations. It therefore seems appropriate to end this chapter by saying something about trust.[2]

One way of bringing out the importance of trust is by

considering language. The possibility of using language to communicate depends on a norm of truth-telling, according to which we accept what others say as true unless we have positive reason not to do so. Consequently, to refuse to accept a person's word for something is to give grounds for offence, and to refuse to accept their word for *anything* is seriously to undermine their status as a language user and therefore as a rational being. (This explains why unease is felt at psychoanalytic practice in so far as it refuses to accept anything the patient says at face value.) To accept what others say is of course to run the risk of being misinformed or misled, since they may be mistaken in what they say or have their own reasons for setting out to deceive. Trust thus carries with it attendant risks which cannot be avoided. On the other hand, trusting others is not the same as being gullible. Bearing this risk in mind, it is sensible to check new information against what is already known and to evaluate it in the light of the informant's reputation for reliability. Being disposed to accept what others say is not inconsistent with a certain degree of scepticism or with a tentative acceptance which is subject, on matters of importance, to further enquiries and investigations.

That communication depends on the acceptance of a norm of truth-telling on the part of both speakers and hearers is indisputable; if someone's saying that it is raining gives no reason for supposing that it is raining then nobody could use language to communicate anything to anybody. It is less clear whether social life generally requires a similar norm of trust. According to Thomas Hobbes (whose view of human nature is a more hard-headed version of Locke's) it does not. In Hobbes' view, the natural state of man is a state of war, since men seek only the satisfaction of their own desires, if necessary at the expense of others. In a state of war, therefore, 'men live without security', 'every man is enemy to every man' and 'force and fraud are . . . the two cardinal virtues'.[3] In such a state there is clearly no room for trust, since no man will keep his word unless he is forced to. Social life based on recognition of shared purposes, leading to joint action based on mutual trust, is not possible. Hobbes nevertheless thought that orderly social life was possible through the creation of a sovereign strong enough to force all others to obey him.

Whether, given his assumptions, Hobbes was right about this does not matter in the present context, since his assumptions have already been rejected. As pointed out in connection with language, trust carries with it risks which cannot be avoided, but it does not follow that we are never justified in taking them. It is true that men sometimes betray the trust which has been placed in them but it is not true that they inevitably do so if they can and as a matter of fact they often do not. Moreover, trust is surely an essential part of what we regard as desirable relations between persons, for example between husband and wife or between parents and children. In general we prefer to trust people if we can, rather than trusting them only when we cannot help ourselves. Indeed, it is inappropriate to speak of trust in such circumstances.

It has been argued that people can be held accountable for what they do only in so far as they are regarded as responsible in the first place. If they were always fully responsible in the senses indicated then trust would always be well-founded. In fact they are not always fully responsible and if we trust them we inevitably run the risk of being let down. It could be argued that without that risk there would be no scope for trust. (If that were the case, and if trust in God *cannot* be misplaced, then it could be argued that trust in God is impossible, since it involves no risk.) Accountability recognises this risk and tries to minimise it. (Since there is no risk involved in trusting God, there is no reason to regard God as accountable for what he does.) It could be argued that to ask for an account is to show a lack of trust. But whether this is true depends to some extent on the circumstances. For a wife to ask a husband what he has been up to may be interpreted as showing a lack of trust, and parents and children often disagree as to how much trust is due to the latter. This may be partly because, as argued earlier, it is appropriate to ask a person for an account only when there is some suggestion that things are not as they should be. In the case of a social entity such as a school, however, the production of accounts may be part of the normal routine and carries no such suggestion with it. Pupils' reports, for example, are intended to report progress, which may be satisfactory or unsatisfactory. Similarly the report of the school as a whole may be intended to draw attention to its successes as much as to any difficulties encountered during the year.

CHAPTER 5 TEACHERS AS OCCUPYING ROLES

A girl was introduced to another guest by the hostess: 'This is Jane who works in social welfare.' Jane immediately denied the relevance of this piece of information: 'Oh don't say that! It's not important what I do but who I am. . . . I'm me, that's what matters.' Other guest: 'Yes, of course, hullo Jane.' There follows a series of grunts, giggles, coughs, visual searches for diverting third parties, and silence. Then, Jane: 'And what do *you* do?' [1]

I. INTRODUCTION

According to the view presented in earlier chapters, teaching is best thought of as a social activity or practice carried on in accordance with a social tradition. Similarly, a teacher is not simply one who tries to help others to learn in ways which involve personal interaction but one who accepts responsibility for doing so as a practitioner in such a social activity. To emphasise the importance of tradition is to draw attention to the fact that the activity of teaching has a continuing identity over a period of time, allowing it to remain the same activity despite changes in the individuals who are its practitioners. So far, however, only incidental recognition has been given to the fact that teaching takes place in highly structured social institutions such as schools, colleges and universities. Typically, a person becomes a teacher, in the sense of a practitioner in the social activity of teaching, by coming to occupy the role of teacher in such an institution. Accordingly, this chapter will be concerned with the nature of roles and the relation between them and their occupants.

A person's role, especially his principal role in life, is an important ingredient in his sense of self-identity, locating, as the quotation at the beginning of this chapter illustrates, his place (or places) in the social scheme of things. So much so, indeed, that to cease to occupy a role especially when, as in retirement, no other positive role replaces it may be highly traumatic and experienced as a diminishment of personality. As such it is an example of the importance, for our sense of being ourselves, of the way others see us. In *Self and Others* R. D. Laing reports a 'growing dissatisfaction with any theory or study of the individual which isolates him from his contexts', especially his relations with others. 'How he perceives and acts towards others, how they perceive him as perceiving them, are all aspects of the "situation".' And he introduces the term 'complementarity' to 'denote that function of personal relations whereby the other fulfils or completes self'.[2] He illustrates this with the example of a little boy who runs to his mother to show her a worm which he has found. She ignores his desire to show her the worm and responds only by saying that he is dirty and telling him to wash. And Laing comments: 'In this tangential response there is a failure to endorse what the boy is doing from his point of view, namely, showing his mummy a worm',[3] thereby diminishing the child as a person with a point of view and interests of his own. As a psychiatrist, Laing is primarily interested in the origins of mental illness in defective social relations. But the idea of 'identity as complementary to others' is of general importance for an understanding of the concept of a person and of persons as occupying roles. What a person *is* depends at least in part on how he sees himself, including how he sees himself as seen by others, which I will call his psychological reality, and also on how he is actually seen by others, which I will call his social reality. As the story about Jane illustrates, the roles we occupy are an important part of how we see ourselves and are seen by others.

II. ROLES AND THEIR OCCUPANTS

1. Roles
Roles may be defined in terms of the duties which they impose and the rights which they confer on their occupants, and they

typically form part of a nexus of related roles which constitute a social institution such as a hospital, school or family.

The duties of the role indicate what its occupant is required to do as occupant of that role and therefore what he is responsible for in the accountability sense. As pointed out in the previous chapter, social institutions such as schools are brought into being for a purpose; accordingly, the duties attached to a role can be expected to reflect that purpose. They are therefore for the most part positive in nature. Unlike a private person, the occupant of a role is expected to *do* something, not merely to refrain from doing things which he should not. A doctor, for example, is responsible for his patient's health, a policeman is required to maintain public order, a teacher has to help others to learn, and so on. Accordingly, in so far as he is accountable, his accountability will be more like that of a social entity than of a person; he will be required to show that he has done his job and not merely that he has done no wrong.

The rights of the role include the privileges, status and income which go with it. More important however are the rights which are internal to the role in the sense of allowing the occupant to carry out the duties associated with it. They authorise him, or give him the authority, to do what needs to be done in order to act effectively in the role; for example, a barrister has the right to plead in court, a doctor has the right to practise medicine, a policeman has the right to make arrests, and so on. Equally a teacher has the right to expect his pupils to attend to what he says and to maintain order in the classroom.

Roles and the social institutions which they constitute thus give structure to social activities such as medicine, the law and teaching. They help to organise the activity by giving definition to the part to be played by particular individuals. The question which has to be considered is how they are able to do this, since it is clear that social roles, practices and institutions all depend on the activities of individual persons for their existence, even although they cannot be identified with those activities. The view taken in Chapter 3, section II, 2(e) was that the members of a profession form a group with a distinct identity primarily because they see themselves as forming such a group; it was argued that if they did not see themselves as doing so then they would not in fact do so. Unlike physical objects such groups depend for being what they are – for their reality – on being seen as what they are, each member of the group seeing both himself and others as members of that group. The members of the group are thus related by what was called reciprocal self-awareness and it is this relation between the members which brings the group into existence.

Roles, which have been defined in terms of the duties which they impose and the rights which they confer on their occupants, come to exist in the same way and have the same kind of reality as social groups. To see oneself as occupying a role is to see oneself as under the obligations which occupancy of the role brings with it and, similarly, as possessing the rights which go with it. In seeing others as seeing you as occupying the role, one sees others as seeing oneself as under those obligations and possessing those rights. This by itself is only psychological or subjective, although real enough in its own way. For a role to be brought into existence it is necessary that the person should also be seen by others as occupying the role and therefore as having those duties and possessing those rights. It is this third re-quirement, that of being seen by others in the relevant way, which confers social objectivity on the person's occupancy of the role and makes him in reality what he supposes himself to be. In short, to occupy a role is to see yourself as occupying that role, to see yourself as seen by others as occupying it and to be in fact seen by others as doing so. This account of what it is to occupy a role relies heavily on the ideas of 'seeing yourself as' and 'being seen as'. Occupying a role therefore involves seeing yourself and being seen in a special light or under a certain aspect, and that aspect involves the possession of duties and rights which attach to the occupant of the role but not to other people.

It might be objected that a doctor, for example, is a person who has qualified as a doctor by passing the relevant profes-sional exams and therefore that the account given above has got things the wrong way round. We see a doctor as a doctor because he is a doctor, just as we see a tree as a tree because it is a tree; it is incorrect to say that he is a doctor because we see him as a doctor. The premise on which this objection is based is certainly correct; doctors do become doctors by passing exams. But, that having been said, something must be said about the exams which have to be passed. The exams concerned must be relevant ones, and that means that they must be set and marked by persons who are authorised to do so, in other words, by persons who occupy the role of examiners. The idea of a qualifying exam therefore takes us back to the idea of a role and so cannot be used to explain it. The fact that a decision about whether to recognise a person as a doctor is taken on the basis of an exam thus complicates the story but does not fundamentally change it. Similar considerations apply to those who come to occupy roles by being appointed, for example as teachers, by others. A teacher becomes a teacher only by being appointed by someone *recognised* as having the authority to do so.

2. *Roles as having a function*

It has been suggested that roles are brought into existence by an implicit social agreement to confer on individuals the duties and rights in terms of which the role is defined. The duties imposed on the occupant of a role in effect require him to do a job which is recognised as socially necessary or useful. The occupant of a role may be said therefore to have a job to do or a function to fulfil. The normal occupant of a role may simply try to perform the duties of the role without giving much thought to its function. He may, however, have some conception of it and may even have ideas about how the role might be modified so that it does what it is intended to do more effectively. The classic example of a visionary in this sense is Florence Nightingale, who by her work changed the whole idea of what a nurse should be.

The idea of the function of a nurse is similar to that of, for example, the carburettor of a car. A car is an artifact constructed for a purpose, that of providing transport. It is able to fulfil that purpose because it consists of parts, such as the engine, gearbox and carburettor, which interact in ways which allow it to do so. Each part makes its own contribution to the efficient working of the stable system which is the car itself. The idea of a thing's having a function is thus different to that of its having rights and duties. A carburettor may be said to have a function but clearly cannot be said to possess rights and duties, and a role, defined in terms of rights and duties, may continue to exist even although it no longer has a function and is therefore obsolete. There can therefore be rights and duties without any corresponding function and a function, like that of a carburettor, which is carried out mechanically and not through the performance of duties and the exercise of rights. What I have suggested, however, is that roles are to be defined both in terms of the rights and duties attached to them and by reference to their function.

It is possible for roles to have this character because they stand in determinate, stable relations to one another and form part of a nexus of related roles which together constitute a social institution such as that of a marriage or school. Indeed, functions can be attributed to things only in so far as they are seen as parts of stable systems. For example, the claim that the function of a carburettor is to regulate the supply of petrol to the engine can be understood only on the assumption that both are part of some more complex system such as a car which was designed for a purpose and that when they function as they should they help the car to fulfil that purpose. It follows that, just as the function of the carburettor is related to that of the engine, the character of any one role in a social institution has consequences for related roles. Indeed it would be more accurate to say that the view taken of the purpose of the social institution itself determines the view taken of the various roles which, together, constitute it. The role of husband, for example, is related to that of wife, the rights and duties involved being in part reciprocal. The husband may be regarded as the hunter or breadwinner, while the wife looks after the home, or indeed vice versa; and the roles of husband and wife are related, although less centrally, to a variety of other roles – the clerk at the registry office, the priest at the church, and so on. How exactly the roles of husband and wife are thought of will depend on the view taken of the purpose of marriage: whether, for example, it is thought of as providing circumstances favourable for the bringing up of children. A school also is a cluster of roles centred around that of the classroom teacher but including also that of headmaster, school caretaker and so on. And the way these roles are thought of will similarly depend on the view taken of the purpose of the school. Even if it is agreed that that is the provision of education, there is room for a great deal of disagreement about exactly what that involves.

The structured situation created by a marriage or a school also includes a place for other persons – in these examples, children in the sense of either offspring or pupils – who, although they may have relevant rights and duties, cannot be regarded as occupying roles. In the same way, a policeman and prosecuting counsel occupy roles but a criminal and a defendant do not; there are many other socially recognised places such as that of patient, inmate, prisoner and client which, although they involve rights and duties, do not constitute roles. The existence of such social places is nevertheless an essential part of the conception of the social institution to which they belong; indeed, the rights and duties attached to the major roles in those institutions relate to them. The rights and duties of teachers, for example, relate primarily to the children they teach.

Pupils, criminals, patients and so on do not count as occupants of roles, even although they occupy well-defined social places which involve rights and duties, because those rights and duties, unlike those attached to roles, do not depend for their rationale on the performance of a job which is recognised as socially useful. Those who occupy them are the recipients of a benefit (or at any rate, in the case of criminals and prisoners, the objects of attention) rather than its providers. They are like the passengers on a bus. The bus driver is there to provide transport, whereas the passengers are not there to make use of it. If there is a demand for transport, for example from a remote country village to the nearest town, then there is a *prima facie* case for providing it. By contrast, if there is a bus service but no demand for its services, perhaps because all the villagers now have cars, then the rational thing to do is close it down. It would be absurd to see this situation as a marvellous opportunity for job creation, employing people to travel backwards and forwards from village to town in order to keep the bus service functioning.

In the same way, whereas teachers have a function to fulfil in relation to pupils, the pupils themselves have no function. It is true that you cannot have a school without both teachers and pupils, but whereas the teachers are there for the sake of the pupils, the pupils are not there for the sake of the teachers. Consider the position of a university failing to attract students. It might be suggested that it should invest in a large number of learning robots, who could do philosophy for three years, then be recycled to study physics or psychology, and so on. Unlike ordinary, common or garden students, the robot students would have a function: they would keep the university going. But the university itself would then have no point.

The absurdity which results when the difference between the position of the occupant of a role and that of its beneficiaries is not appreciated is best illustrated by the following story from *The Book of Heroic Failures* by Stephen Pile. It is entitled 'The Worst Bus Service' and reads as follows: 'Can any bus service rival the fine Hanley to Bagnall route in Staffordshire? In 1976 it was reported that the buses no longer stopped for passengers. This came to light when one of them, Mr Bill Hancock, complained that buses on the outward journey regularly sailed past queues of up to thirty people. Councillor Arthur Chorlerton then made transport history by stating that if these buses stopped to pick up passengers they would disrupt the timetable.' I would like to think that this story is true; it certainly corresponds, if only in part, to my own experience.

3. Roles as objective

To know what a role is is to know, in general, what behaviour is appropriate to the occupant of that role and therefore what behaviour to expect from him or her, whoever they may happen to be. For this reason, the occupant of a role is often compared to the player who puts on a mask or *persona* in order to take part in a play. In some traditions, for example that of the English medieval morality play, the player literally put on a mask of the character he was playing. In the modern theatre of course that does not happen, but in taking part in a play an actor does take on a character other than his own so that the position is substantially the same. We know more or less what to expect from, say, Brutus in *Julius Caesar*, whoever plays the part. What Brutus does in the play depends on the character of Brutus as laid down by Shakespeare, not on that of the player who happens to be playing the part. It does make a difference who plays the part, since individual actors will interpret the role differently; nevertheless they are all indisputably playing the same part.

Just as dramatic parts are played by actors, so also roles in social institutions may be said to be occupied by people. They come to occupy them in a variety of ways, by election, appointment, heredity and so on, either intentionally or involuntarily. But however people come to occupy roles, when they do so it is always possible to distinguish between the person who occupies the role, on the one hand, and the role which they occupy, on the other. A role is thus a kind of social place which is part of the structure of a social institution and, more generally, of social reality. Just as a place in space is to be contrasted with the things which are located in it (otherwise we could not find our way around), a role, as a social place, is to be contrasted with the persons located there. A role has an existence and character which is independent of the particular people who happen to occupy it from time to time. Roles are part of the social reality to which Durkheim drew attention in *The Rules of Sociological Method*: 'When I fulfil my obligations as brother, husband, or citizen, when I execute my contracts, I perform duties which are defined, externally to myself and my acts, in law and custom. And if they conform to my sentiments and I feel their reality subjectively, such reality is still objective, for I did not create them; I merely inherited them through my education.'[5] A role also, like the obligations and duties to which Durkheim refers, possesses an objective reality which is defined independently of whoever happens to occupy it, although as argued in subsection 1 above, it depends on a social consensus or implicit agreement that it exists. It depends, that is, on a shared conception of it as a social place which is or might be occupied by a person and which imposes certain duties and confers certain rights on its occupants. Its character is the character given to it in this way and is therefore given as far as the particular persons who are its occupants are concerned.

Roles thus have a character which is laid down independently of the particular persons who come to occupy them. To occupy a role is to see yourself in a special way or under a certain aspect, the aspect concerned being laid down by the role concerned. It is also to see those who are directly affected by a person's performance in the role in a special way which is similarly determined by the role itself prior to and independently of that person's occupancy of it. For example, teachers not only see themselves as teachers but also see their pupils as pupils, doctors not only see themselves as doctors but also see their patients as patients, and so on. The result is that the occupants of roles see their pupils, patients and so on in ways which are narrowly circumscribed by the role relation and, in turn, are themselves seen by their pupils and patients in ways which are also circumscribed in the same way.

This narrowing of focus is an inevitable consequence of the existence of a role. A teacher is required by his occupancy of his role to concern himself with his pupils' education rather than with their home life. Similarly, a doctor is licensed to concern himself with his patients' health but not with their finances or private sex life. In some cases it could be argued that a concern for a child's education necessitates a concern about his home life or that a concern for a patient's health necessitates a concern about his finances or sex life. But any such extension of the teacher's or doctor's area of concern would have to be argued for, whereas their concern for education and health respectively does not.

Performance in a role thus typically involves relations with other persons, but the persons concerned are required by the role to be seen in a limited, special way. In the same way, roles themselves are occupied by persons who are also seen in a similarly narrow way. This makes it possible for the occupant of a role to cultivate an attitude of detachment – sometimes called professional detachment – from those he has to deal with. In many ways this is an advantage, most obviously in the case of medicine. Clearly if a doctor were affected by the illness and death of his patients in the same way as he would be by that of his family and friends, the burden of the job would become intolerable. On the other hand, the fact remains that both roles and the special social places associated with them are occupied by persons. And a person cannot just be a teacher, or doctor or social worker or pupil, patient or client; he must live a life which has many other aspects. It was for this reason that Jane the social worker, quoted at the beginning of this chapter, said 'It's not important what I do but who I am'. I suggested earlier that this remark failed to recognise the importance to a person of his job. Nevertheless it does contain an important contrast, that between 'what I do' and 'who I am'. Similarly, a doctor in examining a patient will quite properly be primarily concerned with his health, for example with his damaged foot. It would be regrettable if this led him to forget that the foot was attached to a body which belonged to the person sitting in front of him, but wholly unsurprising if his attention was primarily concentrated on that person's foot.

The contrast between what I do (this is, the role I occupy) and who I am (that is, the person I am) raises the question of the relation between what a person does as occupant of a role and what he does in the rest of his life, including what he does in other roles. To be a person is not in itself to occupy a role, although it is to be a candidate for the occupancy of roles. Nevertheless, persons possess rights and have duties which attach to them as persons living in a particular society, in addition to any which they possess as occupants of roles in that society. There is therefore the possibility of conflict between the obligations which the duties of a role impose and those imposed by the more general obligations imposed on a person as a person or as the occupant of other roles. To take a simple example, the duties of a university lecturer include not only teaching but also writing papers and books. Writing can, however, be extremely time-consuming and can easily eat into the time which might otherwise be given to the lecturer's family. The demands made on the same person by the roles of lecturer and of husband or wife can easily lead to a situation in which both sets of demands cannot be met adequately. Conflict can sometimes be avoided by giving up one role or the other but often that is not possible. When the conflict cannot be avoided the person concerned is placed in a dilemma to which there is no one correct solution, but nevertheless he has to decide what to do and to accept responsibility for what he does. He cannot transfer responsibility from himself to his role, since a role cannot be responsible for anything; roles confer responsibility on persons but cannot themselves be responsible. Whatever a person does in such a dilemma he will be liable to criticism but it does not follow that, in taking into account in deciding what to do those considerations which his role or roles require him to take into account, a person is *ipso facto* acting in bad faith; on the contrary, he would be acting in bad faith if he did *not* do so.

4. *Roles and their occupants*

It was argued in subsection 3 above that a role has its own character which is independent of that of the particular persons who happen to be its occupants. It might be compared to a template which is imposed on an originally blank piece of wood or metal to produce a piece of a jigsaw or a key, the same template being used to produce an indefinite number of pieces of jigsaw or keys all of which are identical. Moreover, once produced, the piece of jigsaw or key would fit neatly into the jigsaw or lock for which it was designed, so completing the pattern, just as the occupant of a role is slotted neatly into the social institution to which the role belongs. If this were correct it would follow that one person's performance in a role would be identical with that of any other person, just as the performance of a soldier ant or worker in an ant's nest is identical to that of any other soldier ant or worker. But this comparison is misleading. People are not like blank pieces of wood or metal, waiting passively to receive whatever imprint their roles place upon them. Nor are they like ants, whose position and behaviour in the nest is determined by heredity. On the contrary, they already possess complex personalities and live complex lives. A person's assuming a role is not therefore like a robot's becoming programmed for a particular purpose and then being activated. Each person fills a role in his own unique way, so that although the role remains the same, the events which result from its occupancy will show infinite variety. In the same way it makes a difference which actor plays a particular part in a play, since although the part is the same, each actor is an individual and therefore plays the part differently.

Thus although what a person does as occupant of a role is bound to be dictated in general by the role concerned – a doctor *qua* doctor must practise medicine, a teacher *qua* teacher must teach, and so on – his actual performance will also be the result of other factors. The role itself may be seen in a slightly different way in various hospitals or schools, which often have their own well-marked characters and traditions; being a teacher at Eton is not the same as being a teacher in the East End of London or Harlem in New York. The particular external circumstances which surround a school are also imporant; for example, local social and political factors, the strength of the local teacher's union, the behaviour and composition of the managers, and demographic trends within the catchment area are all bound to circumscribe and influence the behaviour of individual teachers. The most interesting and important factor is still the personality of the person who occupies the role, since roles must be occupied by persons who, as argued earlier, already possess complex personalities which may be both modified by and expressed in the roles which they occupy.

The scope for the expression of personality in the performance of a role varies greatly, depending primarily on how precisely what the person is required to do is laid down by the duties of the role. The worker on a factory production line has little scope for expressing his personality in what he does. He is related to a machine rather than to another person and may even seem to become no more than a part of the machinery himself. The check-out girl in a supermarket similarly does basically the same thing, check out groceries, whatever her personality. If she wishes, however (or if she has been trained to do so) she can respond to customers as one human being to another, recognising their humanity with a smile or a pleasant remark, or she can ignore them totally and talk over them to the girl in the next desk. Thus although her job is concerned with checking out the groceries which people buy, and that in itself is a routine process, there is incidental scope for personal relations. Plus the fact that good personal relations at the check-out point may not only make life pleasanter for everyone but be good business practice as well.

A soldier in a fighting unit such as a platoon is required to work with others as part of his job, but the part which he is required to play in the 'military machine' is determined for him. The wearing of a uniform, for example by a soldier or policeman, is an important way of depersonalising someone's behaviour in the performance of his role, as the word 'uniform' suggests. One soldier wearing a uniform with appropriate insignia and badges of rank is functionally equivalent to another wearing a similar uniform. Military training is in part directed towards this end, by telling the soldier what needs to be done in any situation and getting him to do it in the prescribed way without further reflection. Thus although the job of a soldier requires him to work with others, a systematic attempt is made to depersonalise his relations with them, while enemy soldiers, at least in modern warfare, are wholly depersonalised, being regarded as material to work on rather than as other human beings.

Since to teach is to try to help others to learn in ways which involve direct contact with them, a teacher cannot avoid entering into personal relations with others, and similar considerations apply to doctors and nurses, social workers and the like. The teacher *qua* teacher is interested only in the learning of others but a fuller relation is not ruled out and indeed may be desirable even from that point of view. It was pointed out in Chapter 3, section II, 2 that teaching may be an art rather than a science and therefore that success may depend primarily on the personality of the teacher. Thus although the distinction between a role and its occupant remains, the role of teacher provides considerable scope for the expression of personality. This may be one of the things which attract teachers to teaching. It may also be one of the reasons why some people find it so difficult since, to put it the other way around, teaching makes considerable personal demands. Coming to a *modus vivendi* with a particular class or pupil is thus both an important and a difficult part of the job, a point vividly developed in the book *Blackboard Jungle* and the film, starring Glenn Ford, based on it.

In this subsection I have insisted on the distinction between the person who occupies a role and the role which that person occupies and have drawn attention to the fact that a role has an existence and character which is independent of the particular persons who happen to occupy it. Roles are therefore stable relative to their occupants, who may change while the role itself remains unaltered. It must be recognised, however, that roles themselves and the institutions to which they belong may also change. According to one account, when people get married in the United States these days they sometimes rent not only their apartment but also their furniture. If they then decide they do not wish to remain married, they can part with the minimum of difficulty, simply returning the furniture to the hire company. If this story is true, then it means that the original idea of marriage, with its implication of unreserved commitment, has undergone substantial change. Similarly, the idea that the partners in a marriage should refrain from sexual relations outside the marriage is under pressure. The psychological pressure and loss of orientation which results when the roles of husband and wife change in this way are explored with great sensitivity in John Updyke's novel *Couples*.

The idea of a teacher has also changed in recent years, for

example by the rejection of dinner duty as part of the teacher's normal duties. This could be viewed as an attempt to sharpen the role of the teacher, making it more strictly intellectual and leaving the job of inculcating social behaviour to others. In the same way, as the social climate has changed, the university teacher is no longer thought of as in any sense *in loco parentis* or concerned in any other way with a student's life outside the classroom, with the result that his role also has become more narrowly academic.

5. *Being a person and being the occupant of a role*

Although there may be scope for the expression of personality by the occupant of a role, it remains the case that assignment to a role determines the kind of part which a person plays in a social activity; for example, in the army the sergeant gives the orders and the private carries them out. According to one view however, associated with Jean-Paul Sartre, to submit to the demands of a role is to suffer a diminishment of freedom and, since to be a person is essentially to be free, to suffer a diminishment of personality. According to Sartre there are no objective values and the freedom to choose is a burden from which we cannot escape, and to try to escape from it by pretending that we are not free is to be guilty of bad faith.

In this connection Sartre gives two very well-known examples: that of the girl who pretends not to notice that the man she is with has taken her hand so that she will not have to decide whether to allow him to seduce her; and that of the waiter in a cafe. The waiter is said to be too quick in his movements, too 'solicitous for the order of the customer': 'his gestures and even his voice seem to be mechanisms; he gives himself the quickness and rapidity of things. He is playing, he is amusing himself. But what is he playing? We need not watch long before we can explain: he is playing at being a waiter in a cafe.'[6] The use which Sartre intends to make of these examples is contentious, but on an obvious interpretation the reference to playing is significant. As pointed out earlier, an actor playing a part is required to assume the *persona* of the character he is playing and therefore to suppress his own personality. What he is required to do in the play is decided for him; he himself has to do nothing except play the part.

An actor loses his personality in the part he takes in a play

only for the duration of the play. Sartre's story about the waiter
could be taken to suggest that the occupant of a role may
become so habituated to the role that everything he does is
dictated by it. All his decisions are taken for him; he need decide
nothing. He consequently appears to have denied his freedom
but that is impossible: in fact he has freely decided to be nothing
but a waiter. The idea that an actor might have no existence
apart from the part he takes in a play is explored with great skill
by Tom Stoppard in his play *Rosencrantz and Guildenstern are Dead*.
Rosencrantz and Guildenstern are two relatively unimportant
characters in *Hamlet*. In *his* play, Stoppard looks at them when
they are off-stage, that is, when they are not playing their part in
Shakespeare's play, although they are playing their part in
Stoppard's play. But Stoppard refuses to give them a part, or at
any rate a persona, in his play. Save for their part in Hamlet,
therefore, they are nothing; they live only in and through their
part in Hamlet. As themselves they do not exist; they lack an
identity, as the following quotations show.

GUIL: What's the first thing you remember?
ROS: Oh, let's see. . . . The first thing that comes into my
       head, you mean?
GUIL: No – the first thing you remember.
ROS: Ah. (*pause*) No, its no good, its gone. It was a long time
       ago.
GUIL: (*patiently but edged*) You don't get my meaning. What is
       the first thing after all the things you've forgotten?
ROS: Oh I see. (*pause*) I've forgotten the question.
GUIL: How long have you suffered from a bad memory?
ROS: I can't remember.
       (*Guil. paces*)
GUIL: Are you happy?
ROS: I suppose so.
GUIL: What are you going to do now?
ROS: I don't know. What are you going to do?
GUIL: I have no desires. None. (*He stops pacing dead.*)
[Later Rosencrantz introduces them to the Player.]
ROS: My name is Guildenstern and this is Rosencrantz.
       (*Guil. Confers briefly with him*)
       (*Without embarrassment.*) I'm sorry – *his* name's Guil-
       denstern, and *I'm* Rosencrantz.

[The subject of names come up again later.]
ROS: I remember –
GUIL: Yes?
ROS: I remember when there were no questions.
GUIL: There were always questions. To exchange one set for
       another is no great matter.
ROS: Answer, yes. There were always answers to every-
       thing.
GUIL: You've forgotten.
ROS: (*flaring*) I haven't forgotten – how I used to remember
       my own name – and yours, oh *yes*! There were answers
       everywhere you looked. There was no question about
       it – people knew who I was and if they didn't they
       asked and I told them.[7]

Of course in real life when actors have taken their part in a
play they go home to bed or do whatever they want to do. They
do not find themselves on another stage in a different drama
with no part to play. In other words, when not acting an actor is
a person like anyone else. The suggestion that when they leave
the stage actors simply wait in a formless limbo until it is their
turn to appear on stage again is obviously absurd. The
analogous suggestion that a person is no more than the sum of
his roles is not obviously absurd but, unless made trivially true, is
equally mistaken. It is true if the idea of a role is so extended that
whatever a person does, he is deemed to do it as the occupant of
a role. For example, if he travels on a bus, he does so in the role of
bus traveller; if he plays golf, he does so in the role of golf player;
presumably if he scratches his nose, he does so in the role of nose
scratcher. But though true, it is trivial, since a role is invented for
him to occupy whatever he does. If, however, roles are defined
as involving not only rights and duties but also as having a
function, as described earlier in this chapter, then it is absurd to
suppose that persons always act as the occupant of some role or
other. It might be argued that whatever a person does he does as
a moral agent, since a person cannot become or cease to be a
moral agent through his own or anyone else's decision: he simply
is a moral agent. But to be a moral agent is not to occupy a role,
since a moral agent does not have a function, any more than a
passenger on a bus or a golf player does. We need golf courses
and the services of those who look after them if we are to have

golf players, but we don't need golf players in the same way. We have them simply because people like to play golf. Their playing golf represents the bottom line, and the same is true of the moral behaviour of moral agents. They behave in the way they do because, according to their conception of being human, that is the way to behave. And human life as such has neither point nor function.

6. A comparison with language

It was suggested earlier that to know what a role is is to know, in general, what behaviour is appropriate to the occupant of that role and therefore what behaviour to expect from that person. Many roles, either directly or indirectly, involve relations with other people; for example, that of a doctor, nurse, teacher or social worker. It follows that to occupy a role of this sort is to acquire a ready-made set of relationships with others, complete with instructions on how to behave in that relationship; and the more clearly defined the role, the more complete the instructions will be.

This can be brought out by a comparison with language. Chomsky, among others, attaches importance to the ability of language users to generate wholly new sentences and, correspondingly, to understand the sentences generated by others, even although they have never heard a particular sentence before.[8] This makes it possible for people who have only just met and who know very little about each other to communicate with each other immediately, often about highly complex matters such as last night's football game, provided that they share the same natural language. Communication between people (or indeed animals) who do not share the same language may be possible through the use of simple signs such as pointing, which seem to be universally understood, but what can be communicated in this way is very limited. Beyond that, successful communication, for example in the course of shared purposive activities, will depend on the parties to it coming to know and understand each other as individuals. By contrast strangers who share the same natural language can communicate efficiently straight away even though they may know little or nothing about each other as individuals since in sharing the same language they know a great deal about each other in an impersonal way; for example, anyone who understands English will know what I mean if I say: 'Apple pie and ice cream go well together'.

What makes such communication possible is the existence of linguistic conventions according to which, for example, the words 'apple pie and ice cream go well together' mean that apple pie and ice cream go well together, plus the fact that the parties to it know what those conventions are. Linguistic conventions make possible communication which is impersonal in the sense of not being dependent on the parties to it having prior knowledge of each other. If we wish to be understood we must abide by the appropriate linguistic conventions in saying what we want to say; what we actually say is not determined by the conventions but by what we want to communicate and the circumstances in which we find ourselves. Thus on the one hand conventions constrain us – we must follow them if we wish to be understood – but on the other hand they allow us or make us free to say what we want to say. We are not completely free to say what we like since there may be further conventions which govern what we say. For example, when talking privately with a friend we can say more or less what we want, whereas when attending a religious service we must say what the service requires us to say.

In some respects occupying a role is like sharing a language, facilitating not communication as such but aspects of social life generally. In so far as a role involves relations with others, the structure of those relations is determined, more or less, by the role concerned; the parties to it do not have to set it up for themselves. For example, two soldiers who have never met before know in general how to behave towards one another and work together, even although they have only just met and know very little personally about each other, provided they both hold precisely defined ranks within the same military organisation. The general pattern of their social relations is already defined for them. They do not have to work it out for themselves before they can begin to work together; for example, their respective roles will determine who gives orders and who carries them out. But although the general pattern of their relationship is fixed, the actual transactions between them, for example the particular orders given and obeyed, will be determined by circumstances, just as what we say when we use language is determined by circumstances. Other role relations may be less precisely defined than this. In the case of husband and wife, for example, it may be accepted that the husband is the provider and the wife the homemaker but it is a well-known fact that the parties concerned have to work out a *modus vivendi* for themselves within this framework. In fact the institution of marriage is sufficiently flexible to allow a reversal of these roles, so that their occupancy is not automatically determined by sex.

Roles provide a stable framework of relationships within which people can relate to one another, so that they do not have to start from scratch and do everything for themselves. In many cases, including teaching as well as marriage, that still leaves a great deal to do, allowing at the same time scope for genuine personal relations.

CHAPTER 6   TEACHING, LEARNING AND THE SOCIAL BASIS OF KNOWLEDGE

Bellgrove wakened with a jerk, gathered his gown about him like God gathering a whirlwind and brought his hand down with a dull impotent thud on the lid of his desk. His absurdly noble head raised itself. His proud and vacant gaze settled at last on young Dogseye.

'Would it be too much to ask you,' he said at last, with a yawn which exposed his carious teeth, 'whether a young man – a not very studious young man, by name Dogseye – lies behind that mask of dirt and ink? Whether there is a human body within that sordid bunch of rags, and whether that body is Dogseye's, also.' He yawned again. One of his eyes was on the clock, the other remained bemusedly on the young pupil. 'I will put it more simply: Is that really you, Dogseye? Are you sitting in the second row from the front? Are you occupying the third desk from the left? And were you – if, indeed, it is you, behind that dark-blue muzzle – were you carving something indescribably fascinating on to the lid of your desk? Did I wake to catch you at it, young man?'

Dogseye, a nondescript little figure, wriggled.

'Answer me, Dogseye. Were you carving away when you thought your old master was asleep?'

'Yes, sir,' said Dogseye, surprisingly loudly; so loudly that he startled himself and glanced about him as though for the voice.

'What were you carving, my boy?'

'My name, sir.'

'What, the whole thing, my boy?'

'I'd only done the first three letters, sir.'

Bellgrove rose swathed. He moved, a benign, august figure, down the dusty aisle between the desks until he reached Dogseye.

'You haven't finished the "G",' he said in a far-away lugubrious voice. 'Finish the "G" and leave it at that. And leave the "EYE" for other things . . .' – an inane smirk began to flit across the lower part of his face – 'such as your grammar-book,' he said brightly, his voice horribly out of character. He began to laugh in such a way as might develop into something beyond control, but he was brought up short with a twinge of pain and he clutched at his jaw, where his teeth cried out for extraction.

After a few moments – 'Get up,' he said. Seating himself at Dogseye's desk he picked up the penknife before him and worked away at the 'G' of 'DOG' until a bell rang and the room was transformed into a stampeding torrent of boys making for the classroom door as though they expected to find upon the other side the embodiment of their separate dreams – the talons of adventure, the antlers of romance.[1]

I. THE TEACHER-PUPIL MODEL OF TEACHING

In Chapter 1 two models of teaching were distinguished. According to the horizontal or teacher-teacher model, teaching is a social practice carried on in accordance with a social tradition and according to the vertical or teacher-pupil model, teaching is a species of action rather than a more broadly defined social activity and takes place when a teacher tries to help a pupil or pupils to learn in ways which, typically, involve direct face-to-face interaction between teacher and pupil. The approach adopted in the chapters which followed was that suggested by the first, teacher-teacher model. It was recognised that any account of teaching would be incomplete unless it included a consideration of the specific teaching acts which lie at its heart. Some attention must therefore now be given to them.

According to the definition given above, teaching takes place when a teacher tries to help a pupil to learn in ways which, typically, involve direct face-to-face interaction between teacher and pupil. This is straightforward enough but there are some points which should be made by way of elaboration and clarification.

(*a*) A general assumption behind the definition is that people do lots of different things – more formally, perform different kinds of human actions – in the course of their day: they clean their teeth, feed the cat, make themselves cups of tea and so on. Teaching is just the name of one such kind of action. The most obvious things to say about teaching therefore reflect the fact that teaching is the name of a kind of action. The definition of teaching which has been offered in fact simply replaces that name by a highly general description. Indeed, because that description is so general, it can be correctly applied not only to the teaching acts which lie at the heart of the social practice of teaching but also to acts which have no connection with it.

(b) Since teaching is defined in terms of learning, an account of learning is needed and this will be given in a later section.

(c) To count as teaching the teacher's efforts to help the pupil to learn must involve direct face-to-face contact. Without some such proviso, the proposed definition would be too broad. For example, parents help their children to learn by buying books for them, paying for flute lessons, sending them to fee-paying schools and so on, but it would obviously be incorrect to say that, in doing so, they have taught them anything, even although they have made it possible for them to learn and therefore helped them in this way. Simply providing the means for someone to learn is not enough. In order to count as teaching, there must be at least some direct interaction between teacher and pupil in the actual learning situation. The amount and kind of interaction will vary according to the age of the pupils, the content concerned and many other factors. It may even take place through the medium of the radio, as in parts of Australia, or through the post.

(d) According to the definition, to teach is to *try* to do something. The use of the word 'try' draws attention to the fact that the teacher has some aim in mind in doing what he or she does, that is trying to achieve something. In this respect, teaching is like any other action. The difference lies in what the teacher is trying to do: to bring about learning.

(e) To try to do something is inevitably to take a risk, the risk of failing to achieve what you set out to achieve. The definition requires only that the attempt be made, however, not that it be successful. This is sometimes expressed by saying that teaching is a task word, like 'running in a race', and not an achievement word, like 'winning a race'.

(f) For an act to count as an act of teaching, the teacher must not only have the intention of bringing about learning but must also adopt some method of realising that intention. Like the two previous points, this follows from a perfectly general point about what it is to act. Moreover, the method adopted must be one which seems to have at least a minimal chance of success, although not too much should be made of this last point; it is the intention with which a person acts which is the most important consideration in deciding what he can properly be described as doing.

(*g*) The definition of teaching does not lay down any specific rules as to how learning is or is not to be brought about. Apart from the very general requirement mentioned in (*f*) above nothing is laid down about which teaching methods are to be employed, on grounds either of efficiency or of morals. Inefficient teaching is still teaching, as is teaching which makes use of morally objectionable methods.

(*h*) Again, since to learn is to learn something, it follows that teaching must have some content, but nothing is laid down about what that content is to be. This point was anticipated in subsection 3 of section III, Chapter 3 where it was pointed out that this view of teaching suggests that the question of what the curriculum is to be is entirely open.

(*i*) If teaching is successful, then someone must have learnt something, and to learn something is, in a very broad sense, to have got something right. 'Learning', unlike 'teaching', is a success word. Thus the success of the teacher depends on the success of the learner. That in turn will depend not only on the efforts and skill of the teacher but on many other factors, such as the ability and motivation of the pupil, which lie outside the teacher's control.

(*j*) The teacher can choose a method of trying to bring about learning only if he knows what is to be learnt and therefore what counts as success in learning it. It does not follow, however, that teaching takes place only if the teacher provides the content of learning in the sense of deciding *what* should be learnt. What is to be learnt may be decided by a third party, for example by a government official or a committee of parents, or by the pupil himself, rather than by the teacher. It may indeed be left partly open, being decided in the event by the fortuitous occurrence of favourable opportunities to learn, for example that the bird which has just flown out of a bush is a blackbird.

(*k*) Finally, because the definition is very general, it fails to distinguish between a teacher in the sense of one who accepts responsibility for the learning of others in a regular and systematic way, and one who teaches only occasionally like, for example, a parent who teaches a young child new words. Although teaching is a transaction between two parties, it is thought of as an *isolated* transaction between parties who are not otherwise related; to that extent it is misleading to refer to the parties concerned as a teacher and a pupil respectively.

Each of the points made above could easily be elaborated and spelt out in greater detail but there would be little point in doing so in the present context since, however carefully it was done, the questions which this account of teaching leaves unanswered – about what and how to teach – would remain unanswered. But of course they must *be* answered and some account must be possible of how that is to be done. The form which that account takes will depend on the more general philosophical approach which is being followed. According to the approach adopted in earlier chapters, the account would begin by distinguishing between acts of teaching which are part of a social practice of teaching and isolated acts of teaching which are not. So far as the former are concerned, then the social practice will be carried on in accordance with the guidance provided by a social tradition. So far as the latter are concerned, it may turn out that they also are to be performed as part of a social practice, for example that of child-rearing within the family. If not, then the individual who is doing the teaching really does have to decide for himself, in the light of his own personal plans and wishes, what to do.

If the Lockean approach is followed, a possible reaction to the problem is to elaborate the originally simple definition of teaching in various ways. It might be claimed, for example, that nothing counts as teaching unless methods which appeal to the pupil's rationality or which are acceptable on moral grounds are employed, or that the pupil also should intend to learn what the teacher intends him to learn. The objections to moves of this kind are well known. They can be compared to a conjurer taking a rabbit out of a hat; however baffled we may be by his skill, we are likely to insist that, even if we did not see him do it, he must have put the rabbit into the hat before taking it out again. On the other hand, if this is admitted – if, in other words, the definition is admitted to be stipulative – then reasons must be given why it should be accepted. The most obvious way of doing so would be by reference to an account of education which was itself heavily value-laden. The Peters' account of education mentioned in Chapter 1, for example, includes a reference to 'what is worthwhile'. But it in turn needs to be underpinned by an account of what is worthwhile in the relevant, non-relative sense, and it is hardly question-begging to assert that that cannot be provided.[2] If that is the case then we have no better reason for accepting the proposed definition of education than we had for accepting the original stipulative definition of teaching. In the end the Lockean philosopher of education is driven to a reliance on the *a priori* practical principles which were discussed, and rejected, in section VI, 1 of Chapter 2, where it was pointed out that no satisfactory account could be given of how we come by such principles or of why we should take any notice of them.

II. SPECIFIC TEACHING ACTIVITIES

1. Hirst's claim

Even when all of the points made in the previous section are taken into account the adequacy of the definition of teaching given above can still be questioned. One source of such doubts seems to be as follows. A teacher may say that he has been teaching throughout the afternoon, and if he has been in the classroom and in contact with the children throughout the afternoon his claim seems reasonable. But, as Professor Hirst points out in 'What is teaching?', if 'we look at these more detailed elements of the enterprise, it is perfectly plain that many of them are not activities we would in a more restricted sense of the term wish to call "teaching" at all', for example, sharpening pencils or opening windows. In order to resolve this dilemma he makes a distinction between what he calls teaching as an enterprise and specific teaching activities. 'We talk about teaching as an enterprise', he says, 'in which a person may be engaged for a long period, say all afternoon. In this sense, a teacher spends the afternoon not in shopping, sunbathing or taking the dog for a walk, but in fact in teaching. The term teaching is here functioning at a very general level, labelling a whole enterprise which may be broken down into many specific activities.'[3]

Having made that distinction, Hirst's primary concern is with specific teaching activities. Once they have been identified, a teaching enterprise is one which includes specific teaching activities in addition to the other activities referred to above, in the same way as a currant bun is one which contains a sprinkling of currants, even though it also contains other things. This is unsatisfactory, if only because it provides no way of deciding when a teaching enterprise begins or ends. However, for Hirst the main problem is how 'specific teaching activities [are] to be distinguished from all other specific activities'. He begins by pointing out that 'we characterise specific teaching activities in the way in which we fundamentally characterise all human activities: by looking at their point or purpose' (Hirst, pp. 102, 104). And the purpose of teaching is agreed to be the bringing about of learning. But, even taking into account the proviso that the learning must take place as a result of direct contact between teacher and pupil, this is too wide for Hirst.

One avenue which he explores is that in order to count as a specific teaching activity an action must also satisfy some more specific description such as telling, lecturing, showing, explaining and so on. Something of this sort, he thinks, is the case with gardening, since 'activities like pruning and mowing the lawn are necessarily forms of gardening and that concept can be exhaustively analysed in such terms' (Hirst, p. 104). But he rejects the view that teaching is like gardening in this respect, since, he says, 'none of these activities [that is, telling, demonstrating, proving etc.] implies that teaching is taking place' (Hirst, p. 103). This seems to be correct, since circumstances can easily be imagined in which a person was telling, and so on, even though we would not want to say that they were teaching. Indeed, the point which Hirst makes about gardening is true only in a trivial sense, since for what he says to be correct, terms such as 'mowing the lawn' must be understood in gardening terms. In that case it does indeed follow that anyone who is mowing the lawn is gardening. However, 'mowing' without qualification is not a gardening term; farmers mow grass in fields in order to make hay. 'Mowing the lawn' is a gardening term but only because a lawn is by definition part of a garden. In the same way, there are activities which are necessarily forms of teaching, for example giving lessons, but this is similarly trivial. In any case Hirst is right to reject this approach as a dead end.

He goes on to claim that there are two 'necessary conditions which an activity must satisfy before it could possibly be described as a teaching activity', two 'necessary features of a publicly observable kind which all teaching activities must possess' (Hirst, p. 109). They are that specific teaching activities must indicate what is to be learnt, and that they must do so in a way which makes it possible for the pupil concerned to learn what is to be learnt (Hirst, p. 110). The second feature is little more than a corollary of the first and need not be considered separately. The first claim is intuitively attractive, but as with any philosophical claim the grounds put forward in its support must be assessed. Hirst's reasoning seems to be as follows. He points out that the characterisation of teaching as intending to bring about learning makes the concept of teaching 'parasitic on that of learning' (Hirst, p. 107). He goes on to distinguish between intentional and non-intentional learning and assumes, incorrectly in my view, that only intentional learning is relevant to teaching. He then points out that since learning is intentional it must be directed towards some goal; 'the end or aim of learning', he says, 'is always some specific achievement or end state', such as the acquiring of a new belief, piece of knowledge or skill (Hirst, p. 107). But all that follows from this is that if there is to be such a goal, then *somebody* must set it up as a goal and since the learning concerned is assumed to be intentional, the most obvious person to do this is the person who intends to achieve it, that is, the learner. In this case a teacher is not necessarily involved, although there is no reason why one should not be. If there were a teacher then he would be what was described in Chapter 3 as an agent-for-another rather than a principal, for example like a hairdresser whose customer tells her what she wants done with her hair. Thus it does not follow from the premise that intentional learning must be directed towards some goal that it is the teacher who sets up that goal and then communicates it to the learner. He may as a matter of fact do so but Hirst has failed to show that he *must* set up the goal in order for what he is doing to count as teaching.

What makes Hirst's claim appear so plausible is that, although it is not a logical truth that the teacher must indicate what is to be learnt, it is as a matter of fact true in the contexts in which both Hirst and his readers are interested. They are interested in teaching only in so far as it is part of a social practice of teaching, the purpose of which is connected with education. Given that context, what Hirst claims is correct, but not because of a logical truth about what teaching is. Rather it is a consequence of the fact that learning, whether intentional or not, must have some content and of the fact that, in the learning which is relevant to education, that content must be supplied by some other person. This connection will be considered further in section II, 4.

2. *Flew's claim*

Professor Antony Flew has also put forward an argument about the nature of teaching which, if successful, would require the definition of teaching as trying to help others to learn to be qualified. In a paper called 'Teaching and Testing' Flew puts forward two related theses about teaching. Firstly, he is concerned to 'challenge the assumption . . . that assessment is related to the business of teaching and learning, if it is related at all, only contingently'.[4] Put positively, his claim is that assessment is a necessary part of teaching. Secondly, he endorses the claim, which he attributes to James Andris, that teaching must involve correction as and when necessary, so that, for example, lectures 'given without any arrangements for subsequent feedback' do not count as teaching (Flew, p. 96). In short, Flew argues that (i) assessment and (ii) correction are necessary features of teaching. 'Tests of some sort by which progress can be monitored are an essential of teaching. So too is the checking of whatever deficiencies and misunderstandings may be revealed by these tests' (Flew, p. 96).

Flew bases his claim on the intentional nature of teaching. 'No one,' he points out, 'can be truly said to be acting from some intention unless his actions display at least some minimal consistency with that intention: "It is", as Kai Lung says, "a mark of insincerity of purpose to seek the sacred Emperor in low-class teashops."' 'It is, further, a necessary condition for my sincerity in any purpose that I should be concerned whether, how far, and how well, I am succeeding . . . in that purpose.' 'An authentic teacher', therefore, 'must be concerned with' and take steps to find out whether he is succeeding in his intention of bringing about learning. Flew goes on to conclude that 'assessment and examination in some form are essential to systematic education' (Flew, p. 91).

Thus Flew is making a general point about intentional action as such and then applying it to the particular case of teaching. His general point seems to be correct, although not too much should be read into it. A person performing even the simplest action, such as picking something up, depends on constant visual and proprioceptive feedback about the position of his arm in relation to that of the object being picked up and continually adjusts the movement of his arm on the basis of that information. In the absence of any special explanation we would not allow that a person who did not do so – for example who simply waved his arm around in a random manner – was trying to pick that object up. We would say that he could not be trying to pick it up because he made no appropriate effort to do so. Teaching is much more complex than this but the same principle should apply. In teaching the teacher relies on a constantly changing assessment of how far he is succeeding in getting his point across and, on the basis of that assessment, repeats or rephrases what he has to say, and so on. But the assessment concerned is an assessment of the teacher's own performance, not directly of the progress of the pupil, and it is likely to be based on informal cues of which the teacher himself may not be consciously aware, such as whether the pupils are looking at him, whether they nod in agreement or smile at his jokes or whether they look puzzled or bored. A teacher who is unresponsive to such cues is likely, as we say, to lose contact with the class and, as pointed out earlier, teaching does normally involve direct contact with those being taught.

However, Flew's claim is much stronger than this. In saying that teaching involves assessment he means assessment of the pupil by the teacher. This is made quite clear by his remarks that 'what is ruled out' by his thesis 'is every suggestion of any systematic education freed of all assessment and examination' and that 'the notions of pursuing a course of instruction and of trying to master its contents, without any kind of assessment at all, are simply self-contradictory' (Flew, pp. 89–90). Thus Flew is trying to argue from a purely logical point about the nature of intentional action to a substantive point about educational practice and, moreover, one which is highly contentious.

In considering Flew's claim, it is important to distinguish between two very different uses which are made of tests. Firstly, tests may be used as a teaching device, which help learning by providing the learner with feedback on his progress, thus permitting mistakes to be corrected and errors to be eliminated. In marking essays, for example, it is potentially far more helpful to point out where a student went wrong than simply to give a mark. If a mark is given, the student should ideally be given some indication as to why that mark was given rather than a better or worse mark, so that he can form some idea about what is right and what is wrong with his work. Comparison with the work of other students is not important in this context; the more relevant comparison is with the student's own past performance. Secondly, tests may also be used as an assessment device, the primary purpose of which is to find out what has been learnt. It was pointed out in the previous chapter, for example, that doctors become doctors by passing exams. The purpose of those exams is simply to find out what the candidate already knows in order to decide whether he is competent to practice. Public exams generally – for example O and A levels and final degree exams – are similar. Their purpose is also to find out what has been learnt, with a view to grading either as a basis for future education or for the information of prospective employers or, indeed, of the student himself. Consequently comparison with the standards reached by other students – indeed with as many other students as possible – becomes relevant. Indeed the grades awarded constitute an order of merit rather than an absolute measurement.

The case for regarding tests of the first kind, which provide both teacher and learner with feedback on the learner's progress, as an essential part of teaching is much stronger than that for regarding tests used as an assessment device in that way. Even in their case, I think it would be better to regard their use as a sign of good teaching rather than saying that, in their absence, nothing counts as teaching at all. Flew's main emphasis is on tests of the second kind. In fact he seems to have been inspired (if that is the word) by an article in the *Times Higher Education Supplement* suggesting that university students need not be examined on their work if they elect not to be. But while there may *be* good grounds for grading students by means of public examinations – for example because students or prospective employers want to know how well they have done in comparison with others or as a powerful motivating force for the learning process – there does not seem to be any logical argument, based on a view of what teaching is, for claiming that such exams are essential to teaching. Assessment as such plays little part in, for example, extra-mural or yoga teaching, the main point of which is the intrinsic satisfaction of the student, with no external purpose being served, although correction of understanding or postures is essential if progress is to be made.

There is a further point. Flew maintains, correctly, that anyone who is sincerely pursuing a certain purpose will be concerned about whether, how far, and how well he is succeeding in achieving that purpose. It does not follow, though, that he will necessarily take steps to find out whether he is succeeding. All that follows is that he will have a reason for doing this. But it is easy to imagine cases in which it would not be possible for him to do so. For example, I may make a will with the purpose of ensuring that all my money goes to the cat's home instead of to the undeserving nephew who is my only surviving relative. But however concerned I am to achieve that purpose, it will obviously be impossible for me to take any steps to make sure that I have actually done so, since the directions contained in the will will be carried out, if at all, only after I am dead. Further, it does not necessarily follow that if I have a reason to do something that I will do it, since I may also have a reason not to do it. For example, I may have a reason for cutting the grass, since it will make the garden look neater, but I may also have a reason for not doing so, because I want to get on with writing my book. It does not logically follow that anyone concerned about whether they are achieving a certain purpose, for example that of helping others to learn, will take steps to find out whether they are achieving it. It may not be possible for them to do so and even if it is they may not think it desirable. Whether it is possible to do so depends in part on the purpose concerned. The more narrowly and precisely that is defined, the easier it will be to find out whether it has been achieved. It is relatively easy to find out whether a rat has been taught to press a lever in response to a sound or whether a child has been taught the Lord's prayer. It is less easy to find out whether a child has been taught to appreciate English literature or given the knowledge and skills needed to live a happy and useful life when he leaves school. It could easily be argued that an overemphasis on examinations has a distorting effect on the educational process, leading to a neglect of important but necessarily ill-defined objectives in favour of more narrowly defined objectives which can be stated more precisely.

I conclude that the arguments in favour of assessment in teaching need to be spelt out and balanced against those against. There are two sides to the question, not one, as would be the case if Flew were correct in saying that 'the notions of pursuing a course of instruction and of trying to master its contents, without any kind of assessment at all, are simply self-contradictory'. Flew's view, if accepted, would put a definitional stop on discussion about a matter of great educational importance which is both possible and desirable.

3. Philosophical perspectives on teaching

The feeling that there must be specific teaching activities, which give a teaching enterprise its character *as* a teaching enterprise, is in part a result of an empiricist approach to philosophy such as the Lockean account presented in Chapter 2. A principal feature of empiricist philosophy is its atomistic metaphysic, according to which things which are complex consist of arrangements of simple elements which are the only things which really exist. In order to understand complex things, therefore, it is necessary to analyse them into their simple constituents; hence the method of analysis which is associated with an atomistic metaphysic. This approach is clearly illustrated by the Lockean account of ideas outlined in Chapter 2, according to which the mind comes to be furnished with simple ideas through experience and all other ideas, however complex, consist only of simple ideas joined together in different ways. If we wish to understand any complex idea it is therefore necessary to analyse it into the simple ideas of which it is made up, which are the only things which really exist. The simple ideas themselves are simply given and there is nothing more we can do in order to understand them. A similar view is taken of social groups and activities and of the complex activities of in- dividuals. A teaching enterprise is therefore considered as an example of the latter, to be understood only by analysing it into the specific activities which are, as it were, its atoms.

In opposition to atomism, I have argued that a holistic approach, according to which the parts of complex wholes can be understood only through an understanding of their relation to the complex wholes of which they are a part, offers the only viable approach in social philosophy, including the philosophy of education. In particular, I have argued that teaching is best understood as a social practice carried on in accordance with a tradition and, therefore, that specific teaching activities owe much of their character to their place in such a practice.

III. LEARNING

1. Introduction
Unlike teaching, learning is a topic of great philosophical interest and importance in its own right. It is also of central importance in philosophy of education, since both teaching and education are defined in terms of it.

The ability to learn is not confined to man; many animals other than man possess it to a greater or lesser extent. It is generally accepted, however, that man is outstanding and perhaps unique in this respect, although it might be argued that some animals, for example other primates and porpoises, are comparable. There is, however, no doubt that man is unique in the *use* which he makes of his ability to learn to build up, through the use of language, a cumulative, shared body of knowledge which has transformed his existence and at the same time both created the need for education and made it possible. The next section will be concerned to stress the social nature of knowledge.

From a broader point of view learning is an extension of an animal's ability to survive in a world which is always, in general, hostile. An animal must have a repertoire of behaviours which allow it to respond adaptively to the narrow range of circumstances which constitute its natural environment. Outside that range it is unable to respond adaptively and cannot survive; it will literally be like a fish out of water. But some animals possess the ability to acquire new responses as and when they are needed and so to some extent are able to extend the range of circumstances in which they can survive. Responses which are acquired in this way may be described as learnt responses, in contrast with the instinctive reponses which were part of the animal's original genetic endowment.

Defined in this way, learning includes a very wide range of phenomena, not all of which are of direct interest to the philosopher of education; many different kinds of learning have been distinguished by psychologists, including classical and operant conditioning, trial and error learning, insight learning and latent learning, some of which will be mentioned later. From the present point of view perhaps the most helpful distinction to be made is that between cognitive and non-cognitive learning. Cognitive learning may be defined as learning which results in the formation and modification of beliefs and is therefore possible only for creatures capable of holding beliefs. This includes many animals other than man but does narrow the field down substantially; in particular it excludes conditioning, which has very little to do with education. Cognitive learning, and its connection with a further important distinction, that between direct and indirect learning, will be considered later in this section, in subsection (c). A further distinction, which was anticipated in section II, can be made between intentional and non-intentional learning. It is often thought (by Hirst and Flew among others) that only intentional learning is relevant to education, but this must be a mistake. Children, very often, creep unwillingly to school, and when they go willingly they do so for many reasons other than the desire to learn; for example because they wish to meet their friends or because they like the teacher. They may therefore intend to learn but on the other hand they may not; it is not, that is, logically *necessary* for them to do so in order for it to be possible to say that they do in fact learn. Indeed it seems rather to be the case that many of the difficulties and stresses of teaching are created because children do not wish, or therefore intend, to learn what the teacher wants them to learn. It could of course be argued that it is *desirable* that children and students should intend to learn rather than having learning imposed upon them, both on grounds of efficiency and out of respect for their autonomy as self-determining individuals, but that is another matter.

2. *Learning as learning by experience*

According to Locke's account of the acquisition of ideas, all simple ideas are acquired through experience; that is, by our coming into contact with the world through our sense organs and, as a result, finding out about the world and so being able to make our way about it. In the same way learning is finding out about the world through experience of it. As a matter of logic, all learning is learning by experience. In the *Meno* Plato puts forward a view of learning as reminiscence, that is, remembering what was already known in a previous life, but Locke's is the only plausible theory from a modern scientific point of view.

What this view amounts to can be brought out by contrasting learning with its main conceptual rival, development. Learning and development are similar in that both involve change in the beliefs or behaviour of an animal or child, normally of an adaptive kind, over a period of time; in both cases the change which takes place is a function of external as well as internal circumstances. In the case of development, external circumstances can frustrate the process to a greater or lesser extent, so that it either does not take place or does so only partially. The direction of change, however, is always laid down by the kind of thing concerned. In favourable circumstances acorns grow into oak trees, but however favourable the circumstances they never grow into anything but oak trees. Learning also can be frustrated by circumstances, for example by extremes of heat, cold or tiredness. But, in contrast to development, the direction of change is determined by external circumstances as experienced by the learner. Thus the way an animal or person – or indeed a plant – develops is determined by the kind of thing it is; whereas what an animal or person learns is determined by its experiences. However, although the concepts of learning and development are to be contrasted in this way, in the life of an animal or child they complement one another and proceed side by side. For example, skills can be learnt only when the development of the necessary muscles and neural connections make it possible, and, most importantly, the ability to learn itself develops as children get older, a connection which is reflected in the concept of mental age.

Although all learning is learning by experience, not all experiences which lead to a change in belief or behaviour count as learning experiences, even if they are adaptive or advantageous in some way. Suppose, for example, that a man came to know that bee stings are painful as a result of being hit on the head with a mallet or became a good mathematician as a result of eating toffee, and so on; then he could not be said to have learnt that bee stings are painful or how to do mathematics, even although he would have come to know that bee stings are painful or had become a good mathematician. This is because, although relevant changes in belief and behaviour occurred and did so as a result of experience, the experience concerned was not of the right kind. That this is so is intuitively obvious; indeed the examples seem silly, since it is obvious that things do not happen like that. But it is not easy to say why this is so. Roughly, it is because there is no intelligible connection between the experience which brought about the change and the change itself, although if the facts were as stated there would presumably be a causal connection of a mysterious kind. It would be mysterious not simply because we cannot see how being hit on the head with a mallet could produce the belief that bee stings are painful, or how eating toffees could change a person's behaviour, but because even if it did there is no reason whatsoever why beliefs produced in this kind of way should be true or the behaviour in any way adaptive or skilled.

In an earlier paper I have tried to express this more precisely by suggesting that in learning the relation between the experience which brings about the learning and the learning which is brought about by it must be internal in that the description of what is learnt and of the way in which it is learnt must overlap in containing the same propositional core; for example, one may learn that bee stings are painful by being stung by a bee and finding it painful or, indeed, by being told that they are.[5] However it is expressed, it is clear that something like this is essential to the concept of learning. This is not an arbitrary stipulation. It is connected with the fact that we use the concept of learning to talk about the ways in which we come to know about and to be able to cope with the world we live in through our experience of it; in other words, with the fact that learning is an epistemological concept. We are able to acquire knowledge and skill through our experience of the world because that experience is primarily a function of the way the world is. Consequently in general what we learn is that things are as we experience them. Our experiences can mislead us, since our experience of the world is not a direct mirror image of the way the world is, as the Lockean story suggests. It depends on a way of seeing which, in being selective, provides scope for misclassification; our sense organs may be less than perfect, and abnormal circumstances may lead to a distortion of our perceptions. But unless things were as we experience them, at least normally, we could not rely on our experiences to acquire knowledge of the world and skill in dealing with it, and in that case it would be difficult to see how we could have any such knowledge or skill at all. We can make sense of the suggestion that a man might come to know that bee stings are painful as a result of being hit on the head with a mallet, but only as an aberration from the normal course of events.

3. Direct and indirect learning

If the view that all learning is learning through experience, as so far understood, were correct then the amount which any one animal or person could learn would be restricted to what that person could experience. Since life is short and we can only be in one place at a time that would be very little and, for the most part, would be of only passing and local importance. Each individual would have to accumulate his own store of knowledge about the world and when he died his painfully accumulated stock of knowledge would die with him. Yet that is very far from being the case, at least as far as people are concerned. We know about many things of which we have had no experience; we know, for example, that arsenic is poisonous, that the air is very thin at high altitudes, that it is cold and dark in the depths of the ocean and so on. We can know about the geography of distant continents or the other side of the moon and about the life style of long dead peoples. In fact, most of what we know we do not know by experience at all, or at least not directly so; we know it only indirectly on the authority of others.

Although this is undeniably the case, there is a temptation to dismiss it as philosophically unimportant and to emphasise instead the epistemological primacy of direct experience. Philosophers such as Locke, who are primarily interested in the foundations of knowledge, have traditionally concerned themselves with what can be learnt directly from experience plus what can be inferred from it, presumably on the grounds that what is learnt indirectly from somebody else must have been learnt at an earlier stage by that person. If they in turn learnt it indirectly then somebody else must have learnt it, directly or indirectly, and so on until the chain is brought to an end with somebody who learnt it directly. Thus authority is listed as a source of knowledge, if at all, only to be quickly dismissed, and it is implicitly suggested that each individual has to find out everything he needs to know about the world for himself. While this may be true of animals which are not able to communicate, it is not true for those who are. This view will be criticised in the next section as being wholly inadequate for an understanding of the organised knowledge which is the product of systematic enquiry. Moreover, the philosopher of education is interested in the transmission of knowledge rather than its foundations and cannot afford to dismiss indirect learning so easily.

In order to benefit from the learning of others, an animal or person must have some way of finding out what they have learnt, and the most obvious way of doing so is by receiving a communication from them.[6] The thesis that all learning is learning by experience is still preserved. The learner experiences the communication directly but the original experience only vicariously through the medium of the communication; the experience concerned, that of receiving the communication, is still of the relevant sort. There is no difficulty in seeing how somebody could learn that it is raining outside by being told that it is raining. The knowledge gained by the learner is based on authority – the authority of the person from whom the communication is received. And the knowledge concerned is now shared by both of them.

The idea of communication is sometimes used very broadly to include the various ways in which animals and birds influence the behaviour of other members of their own species, for example, the cry used by blackbirds to warn their young of danger. But it is fairly obvious that the mother blackbird does not intend to warn her chicks; in making her cry she is simply responding directly to the presence of danger. The chicks also respond directly to the cry by taking cover. The mother bird does not have a belief – that danger is present – which she intends to communicate to the chicks, nor do the chicks acquire such a belief as a result of her cry, even though their behaviour is influenced in ways which, on the whole, are adaptive. Any learning which takes place is therefore non-cognitive. Behaviour of this sort is in some ways similar to the so-called body language to which Desmond Morris has drawn attention. There is a sense in which we all give off messages about ourselves and our attitude to others by the way we hold and move our bodies, the direction of our gaze and perhaps even by the smells which we emit, to which others respond in predictable ways, even though neither we nor they are aware of doing so and certainly do not intend to do so.

Signals of this sort are clearly of great importance in the lives of animals of all kinds, especially in bringing about the synchronisation of behaviour necessary for sexual reproduction, and may have provided the biological basis needed for the development of language. But they differ substantially from the words of a natural language such as English. Firstly, the signals, in so far as it is correct to say that they mean anything, have only one specific meaning, like pictorial road signs. Unlike words, they cannot be joined together in accordance with syntactical rules to form other signals which have a new and more complex meaning. Secondly, they are limited in the kind of information which they provide, which is for the most part related only to the immediate circumstances in which the signal is emitted. A message like 'Look out – there is a cat creeping up behind you', although of great present importance, is soon out of date and could not contribute to the formation of a body of shared knowledge of permanent usefulness and interest. Thirdly, unlike linguistic communications, signals such as the warning cry of a blackbird are not produced intentionally; they are simply a direct response to present circumstances. Finally, they seem to be innate and specific to the species; unlike language they are unlearnt and do not depend on convention.

I have been assuming that blackbirds do not possess beliefs and intentions, and this assumption is clearly correct as far as many of the creatures which influence each other's behaviour through their signals are concerned, such as ants and bees. It is not justified in the case of all animals, however, including that of the chimpanzee and of ourselves. Such a creature may have beliefs not only about its surroundings but also about other members of its own species. In particular, it may realise that they also have beliefs and intentions, like itself. In that case there is no reason why it should not set out to communicate its own beliefs and intentions to others. The most obvious way of doing so would be by intentionally producing the sort of signal which it had previously produced only automatically, such as the chattering response of a monkey to a predator. Once communication had been established in this way, making conscious, intentional use of innate signals such as smiles and gestures, the development of language would become possible. Until that development took place, communication would be at best limited and would depend for its success on personal familiarity between the parties to it, since each person would try to communicate in the way he happened to think best. Conventions would then gradually grow up, requiring the same symbols to be used in a similar way by everyone.

The existence of a shared language allows any two language users to communicate easily and reliably, even about complex matters, even though they have never met before and know very little about each other. (This point was elaborated earlier in Chapter 5, section II, 6.) It also greatly facilitates the growth of a shared public body of knowledge which is impersonal in the sense of being the common property of a community rather than of any one individual, and so allows the collective experience of one generation to be passed on to the next. This process is intensified with the invention of written language which allows information to be stored objectively (that is, elsewhere than in the minds of individuals) and even lost and subsequently retrieved.

I said earlier that in order to benefit from the learning of others an animal or person must have some way of finding out what they have learnt and that the obvious way of doing so is through some form of communication. There is one other way of doing so which is worth mentioning, and that is through imitation. Imitation, like communication in the narrow sense, is possible only for creatures which possess beliefs and intentions. It can be illustrated by the following example. A colony of Japanese macaque monkeys living on a sandy beach were fed with rice. For a long time rice which fell on the sand could be retrieved only by picking it up, tediously, a grain at a time. One day, however, one monkey threw a handful of sand and rice into the sea and discovered that the sand sank to the bottom leaving the rice floating on the surface. Whether this initial discovery was made by chance or was the result of some special insight does not matter here. What is relevant is that other monkeys soon followed the example of the first, thus learning indirectly a new way of separating rice from sand. In doing so, they learnt by experience, but their experience was that of seeing and understanding what the monkey responsible for the original discovery was doing. They could not have done this unless they saw it as a model which they also might follow; and they could not have done that, in turn, unless they saw it as having beliefs and intentions like themselves.

The interpretation I have placed on this particular example might be disputed but that does not undermine the conceptual possibility to which it draws attention. It is reasonable, indeed, to suppose that learning of this specially sophisticated sort played a part in the development of the linguistic conventions mentioned earlier. If other people observed one particular person succeed in communicating by employing a certain gesture or making a certain sound, and on the basis of that observation went on to use the same method in order to communicate the same thing, then it is easy to see how first a social habit and then a social convention, laying down how that communication should be made, might grow up. It is also easy to see how a group living together, such as a colony of macaque monkeys, might acquire a shared stock of knowledge through imitation and thus in the course of time acquire a way of life, or way of seeing and doing, which was peculiar to that group, and perhaps even a sense of its own unique history. It is to be expected indeed that something of this sort would happen if the chimpanzees who have been taught American sign language are allowed to form a breeding colony, not only communicating with each other but also teaching their own offspring to do so from infancy.

4. Learning and teaching

In section II, 1 I drew attention to Professor Hirst's suggestion that specific teaching activities must be indicative of what is to be learnt in such a way that it becomes available to the learner. Since then it has been argued that all learning is learning by experience and that the experience must be of the appropriate kind, and that the direction of change which occurs in learning is determined by external circumstances as experienced by the learner. Looked at slightly differently, the change which occurs in learning can also be seen as the content of that learning. The content of learning is therefore directly related to the circumstances which bring it about, as in the example of the man who learnt that bee stings are painful by being stung by a bee. Thus we learn about the world through coming into contact with it, and what we learn is that the world is as we experience it. Hirst's claim can now be paraphrased as follows: the learner's situation, as experienced by the learner, provides the content of what is to be learnt, although it can do so only if the learner is sensitive to situations of that kind. Thus a man may learn that bee stings are painful as a result of being stung on the nose by a bee, but only provided he is not on the way home from the dentist with his face still anaesthetised.

Hirst's procedure was to combine an account of learning with a definition of teaching as intending to bring about learning and, although the way in which that procedure was followed was criticised, the procedure itself was sound. It is therefore worth trying to combine what has now been said about learning with the same definition of teaching. It follows from what has been said about learning that a learner can learn something only if given the opportunity to do so. Therefore the most obvious way of trying to help someone to learn is by providing them with that opportunity. It does not follow that, once the opportunity has been provided, learning takes place automatically. It may do so; the man who had the opportunity of learning that bee stings are painful was undoubtedly taught a lesson which he could not easily ignore. Yet in other cases the mere opportunity, although necessary, may not be sufficient to ensure learning. Neither a child nor a chimpanzee can learn to speak English unless given the opportunity of doing so, but only the child will in fact learn to do so. In other cases, the learner may have the ability to learn something but only with difficulty, and such difficulties provide further scope for a teacher to help bring about learning. In order to do so he will have to adopt some method, the choice of method depending primarily on what has to be learnt and who has to learn it. Nothing further can be said about the methods to be used in teaching simply on the basis of a consideration of what constitutes either teaching or learning.

IV. THE SOCIAL BASIS OF KNOWLEDGE

1. *Locke's epistemological individualism*

The principal aim of this section is to establish the social basis of the kind of knowledge which is relevant to teaching and education. The theory of knowledge which stems from Locke and Descartes is highly individualistic and the position of each will therefore be briefly reviewed.

According to the Lockean view outlined in Chapter 2, each individual has to build up a picture of the world through his own direct, personal experience of it. Men use language to communicate thoughts to others but in doing so they are simply giving outward expression to thoughts which are already fully formed. Language is necessary for the communication of knowledge but plays no part in its formation. Thus men do learn indirectly from the experience of others but such learning is philosophically uninteresting, since knowledge cannot originate in this way and for Locke it is the foundations of knowledge which are important.

The use of the term 'foundations' in this connection reflects a two-tier view of the structure of knowledge based on an analogy with the foundations of a building and what is built on those foundations. The foundations of knowledge are provided by experience but our knowledge can be extended beyond those foundations by the use of inference. Thus we know some things directly through experience and others indirectly through inference based on that experience. For example, Robinson Crusoe saw footsteps in the sand and went on to infer from this that there were strangers on the island. Giving an acceptable account of inferences of this kind has been seen as a problem for empiricism, the so-called problem of induction, since they are admittedly not deductively valid. (There would be no formal contradiction in admitting the existence of the footprints but denying the presence of strangers on the island.) That problem need not detain us here. The point is that, in so far as knowledge can be extended beyond experience in this way, each individual can do so for himself, without help from anyone else, as did Robinson Crusoe. It is still the case that the individual builds up his own picture of the world based on his own experience of it plus the inferences which he makes on the basis of them.

2. *Descartes' first person account of the basis of knowledge*

Locke's epistemological individualism, although not his emphasis on experience, was also shared by Descartes. In Part One of the *Discourse on Method* Descartes describes his education at the Jesuit college of La Flèche in Maine. 'I was studying in one of the most celebrated schools in Europe,' he says, and 'had been taught all that others learned there.' 'But', he goes on, 'as soon as I had finished the entire course of study I found myself involved in so many doubts and errors, that I was convinced I had advanced no further in all my attempts at learning, than the discovery at every turn of my own ignorance.' He was thus led to conclude 'that there was no science in existence that was of such a nature as I had previously been given to believe'. 'For these reasons,' he tells us, 'as soon as my age permitted me to pass from under the control of my instructors, I entirely abandoned the study of letters and resolved no longer to seek any other science than the knowledge of myself or of the great book of nature.'[7]

Later Descartes developed his famous method of doubt, resolving to reject as false anything which he found it possible to doubt. He found it possible to doubt the existence of the external world, including that of his own body, since he could not be sure that he was not dreaming. Even the truths of mathematics, such as that the angles of a triangle add up to 180 degrees and that two and two are four, fell under suspicion, since he might be being deceived into accepting them by a malignant demon. He found, however, that he could not doubt that he was thinking, since to doubt is to think and such doubts are therefore self-refuting. He concluded that he could not doubt his own existence as a thing that thinks. This of course is his celebrated cogito argument: I think, therefore I am. His knowledge of his own existence thus provided the first principle of knowledge which he was seeking. On the basis which it provided he went on to prove, at least to his own satisfaction, the existence of God and of the external world. Thus in his view also knowledge has a two-tier structure, with the truths provided by the cogito argument and the proofs of the existence of God providing a foundation on which the rest of knowledge has to be built.

The autobiographical way in which Descartes presented his arguments was not merely a matter of style; it was essential to the arguments themselves. He used the cogito argument to show that he, himself, existed, but at best it does nothing whatsoever to show that anybody else exists. Anyone who wishes to use it to reassure himself of his own existence must do so for himself. 'You think, therefore you exist' is just as valid as 'I think, therefore I exist' but does nothing to establish your existence, since the premise 'you think' has not been established. In other words, the argument rests on the assumption that thought is self-illuminating to its possessor, so that if I think I cannot but know that I do so, but it is completely hidden from everyone else. You are in a position to know that you think just as I am in a position to know that I think; but I am not in a position to know that you think nor are you in a position to know that I think.

In the Cartesian view the mind is characterised by thought, and thought is private to its possessor. (Both of these views were shared by Locke. In introducing them by reference to Descartes I am simply following a well-established convention of associating them primarily with Descartes.) It follows that in order to establish the existence of other people, which is obviously something which can be doubted, Descartes had first to prove that the external world existed and that its contents included bodies similar to his own; he had then to go on to prove that those bodies were related to minds in the way in which his body was related to his mind. As a matter of fact he does not seem to have seen the need to do so himself. Since his time, however, and especially since the growth of the social sciences, it has been recognised that there is a problem here, the so-called problem of our knowledge of other minds, and attempts have been made to solve it by some form of argument from analogy. Whether any of these attempts have been successful, or whether indeed the problem is soluble on its own terms, need not concern us here. The point is that in Descartes' view, whereas our knowledge of

ourselves provides the basis of all other knowledge, no importance is attached to knowledge of other people, which comes, if
at all, only after knowledge of the external world.

Thus Descartes not only shared Locke's two-tier view of
knowledge but also his individualism, about which he is in fact
much more explicit than Locke. In Part II of the *Discourse* he
points out that towns which are planned by a single architect are
superior to those which have simply grown haphazardly. 'There
is', he says, 'seldom so much perfection in works composed of
many separate parts, upon which many different hands have
been employed, as in those composed by a single master.'
Applying this to the sciences, he concludes that 'the sciences
contained in books, . . . composed as they are of opinions of
many different individuals massed together, are further re-
moved from truth that the simple inferences which a man of
good sense using his natural and unprejudiced judgement draws
respecting the matters of his experience.'[8] Thus Descartes
rejected social or shared knowledge in favour of personal
knowledge – the knowledge which one person, acting alone, can
acquire for himself. Indeed he thought that once he had
discovered the right method he himself, working alone, would
be able to complete the task of scientific enquiry within his own
lifetime.

3. *Common sense knowledge*

So far, in opposition to Locke and Descartes, it has been pointed
out that if all learning were learning directly through experience
and the inferences based on it, then the amount which any one
individual could learn would be very limited. Yet in fact one
person can communicate what he has learnt, on the basis of his
own personal experience, to others and much human knowledge
is therefore social in the sense that it has been acquired from and
thus come to be shared with others. This allows the stock of
information available to any one individual to be much greater
than it would be if each person's knowledge were confined to
what that person had learnt directly. This means that over a
period of time a community of people can build up a stock of
common sense knowledge, each generation adding to what has
been handed down by the previous generation. When this
happens the identity of the person who originally made a certain

discovery is likely to be lost in the mists of time, so that for all practical purposes everybody learns it from somebody else.

The contents of common sense are likely to be both extensive and varied. It includes things which are immensely important to man, although so familiar as to be taken totally for granted, like the knowledge of how to control and make use of fire and of the principle of the wheel. It also includes a ragbag of beliefs and opinions, many of which would not bear examination and are really no more than superstitions. Thus although common sense is what everybody is assumed to know, the use of the word 'know' cannot be taken too seriously in this context, since there is widespread philosophical agreement that mere belief is unsufficient for knowledge. In order to count as knowledge, what is believed must not only be true but must have been established as true by a critical examination of the evidence for it. Common sense beliefs do not measure up to these requirements. Some of them are not even true and even those that are tend to be accepted uncritically on the authority of the anonymous past. Moreover, every time a belief is passed on, there is a risk of distortion and the more often it is passed on the greater the distortion is likely to be. This can be illustrated by serial retelling experiments in which the experimenter tells a story to one person, who then tells it to another and so on, until the last person in the series tells it back to the experimenter, who is then in a position to compare the story as told to him by the last person in the series with the story which he told to the first person. Such experiments confirm that substantial systematic distortion does in fact occur. Common sense beliefs are similar except that there is of course normally no possibility of comparing the present belief with the original, save in a very few cases; for example, successive drawings of plants, each based on its predecessor, were made during the middle ages, all based on the same original drawings of actual plants which were made in ancient times. The drawings became more and more stylised and less and less like the plants they were intended to represent as they were increasingly based on drawings and drawings of drawings rather than on observation.

Thus reliance on common sense knowledge (as I will continue, for the sake of convenience, to call it) has the advantage of allowing the benefits of experience to be shared but also has the disadvantage of being unreliable and leading to error. According to the philosophical principle known as Occam's razor we should minimise the risk of error by accepting as little as possible on the authority of others, relying instead on direct personal experience. Putting it in a more familiar way, don't take anybody else's word for it, see for yourself. In some circumstances this is clearly good advice, for example when buying a second-hand car, but if followed generally it would mean that the advantages of benefiting from the experience of others would also be lost. However, with the rise of the various branches of systematic enquiry a way has been found of allowing reliance to be placed on the accumulated experience of others while avoiding the unreliability built into common sense. Here I will use the example of physical science, although there are of course other systematic enquiries, including mathematics, history and the social sciences.

4. Systematic enquiry

Science can be thought of as a social practice carried on in accordance with a tradition although its overall purpose is not practical, like that of painting and teaching, but theoretical. It is to enquire into and to try to understand and explain the physical nature of the world we live in. In pursuing that purpose, it is guided by a tradition of enquiry which determines, among other things, what counts as a scientific discovery or an addition to scientific knowledge. Claims to have added to scientific knowledge must be subjected to the scrutiny of the community of scientists concerned with such knowledge before they are accepted. Nothing counts as knowledge in this systematic sense unless it has been checked and passed by those authorised and competent to do so. A person becomes an authority in this sense by being recognised as an authority by the rest of the scientific community, each of whom also became an authority, to a greater or lesser degree, in the same way. The existence of a scientific community thus depends on reciprocal self-awareness in the same way as any other social group.

It follows from this that scientific knowledge has a social character very different from that supposed by Descartes. He could not have completed the task of scientific enquiry on his own if only because science, of its very nature, must be the work of a community of scientists rather than of one man. It follows also that scientific knowledge must be shared – if only with other scientists – since nothing counts as scientific knowledge unless established inter-personally. In this way the uncertain quality of common sense is remedied not by a retreat to the individual but by a greater and more orderly reliance on others. This is reflected in the emergence of scientific societies (including the Royal societies which were founded in Descartes' own day), correspondence (of the kind which Descartes himself engaged in with his contemporaries), journals, conferences and so on. To be taken seriously, alleged discoveries must be accompanied by an account of the methods used to make them, thus making it possible for others to check them. The primary purpose of publication is therefore to allow claims to scientific knowledge to be evaluated rather than to disseminate knowledge already recognised as such to be disseminated. Evaluation is part of the process of enquiry, not something subsequent to it, since nothing counts as knowledge unless it is recognised as such. Although individuals are credited with the making of enquiries scientific knowledge is necessarily shared from its inception. Thus scientific knowledge is a social phenomenon in the sense indicated earlier; it exists only in being perceived to exist by the scientific community. It does not follow, of course, that the phenomena studied by scientists are social phenomena. Trivially, physical scientists study physical phenomena, chemists study chemical phenomena, and so on, and physical and chemical phenomena are not social phenomena.

I would like now to consider some possible counter-examples to the thesis that nothing counts as scientific knowledge unless it has been validated inter-personally. It is reasonable to suppose that Captain Nemo, the master of the *Nautilus* in Jules Verne's novel *Twenty Thousand Leagues under the Sea*, made many scientific discoveries in the course of building and equipping his unique submarine. In which case he did not pass them on to anyone, yet this did not prevent the submarine designed in accordance with them from working. Similarly, in Mary Shelley's well-known novel, Dr Frankenstein discovered the secret of life, thus allowing him to create his famous monster but, appalled by what he had done, he refused to reveal the secret to anyone.[9] Again, in real life the scientist Cavendish made many important discoveries but, living as he did the life of a recluse, he communicated them to no one and they remained unpublished until after his death.

What these examples show is that it is perfectly possible to imagine the possibility of discoveries which, if not scientific because not shared and validated by others, are otherwise identical with scientific discoveries; the last example shows that this sometimes actually happens. This might be thought to suggest that the thesis depends on an arbitrary stipulation which refuses to allow anything to count against it. But the stipulation is not arbitrary and it is not mine, it is that of the scientific community. Cavendish was not recognised as a great scientist until his discoveries were confirmed by others after access had been gained to his papers after his death; until that happened there was no way of knowing that he was a great scientist and not just a crank or a Casaubon. Captain Nemo and Dr Frankenstein both gave others reason to suppose that they had made important scientific discoveries since in making their submarine and monster respectively they showed that they could do things which no one else knew how to do, but neither could be credited with making any scientific discoveries until the discoveries themselves were made public and confirmed. Until then the attitude of the scientific community would be one of extreme scepticism, as it was to a recent claim to have cloned a man.

Even if the thesis is accepted, however, it might be pointed out that scientific knowledge still rests on the investigations of the individuals who make the original discoveries. The history of science is after all the history of the achievements of the great men of science – Newton, Harvey, Pasteur, Watson and Crick and the rest – just as the history of painting is the history of the achievements of Leonardo, Giotto and Constable. But while this is true, it is also true that an individual can claim to have made a discovery only in the context of a tradition of enquiry, a tradition to which he belongs and in which he has a place but which exists independently of him and his part in it. Sir Karl Popper puts it as follows: 'A scientist engaged in a piece of research, say in physics, can attack his problem straight away. He can go at once to the heart of the matter; to the heart, that is, of an organised structure.'[10] Before engaging in research a scientist must therefore find out what is already accepted as scientific knowledge, what methods must be employed in adding to it and, above all, what the current 'problem situation' is; in other words, he must become educated as a scientist. As a matter of logic none of these things can be learnt directly from nature; they can be learnt only indirectly from other scientists who know them already and from the 'objective' store of knowledge, such as books, referred to earlier. Even the making of discoveries is therefore part of a co-operative enterprise which looks to a history of previous enquiry as well as to the future. Thus it is the knowledge inherited from the past which provides the real foundations of future knowledge, not the private experiences of isolated individuals, just as it was what Taddeo inherited from Giotto which allowed him to improve on Giotto's colouring.[11]

In this subsection I have been concerned to draw attention to only one aspect of the tradition of scientific enquiry, its insistence on open, public validation procedures. But, as pointed out in Chapter 2, the guidance which a tradition provides includes not only a way of doing but also a way of seeing. Brief mention ought therefore to be made of the way of seeing provided by science. The overall purpose of scientific enquiry is not, or not simply, to describe the physical character-istics of the world we live in but to understand and explain them, and this is done primarily by providing new and increasingly abstract ways of seeing or conceptualising things. This allows theories to be developed which present phenomena which to ordinary experience seem unconnected as manifestations of the same underlying structure and as obeying the same laws. As science progresses its way of seeing increasingly departs from our ordinary way of seeing things and its validation procedures become increasingly complex and remote from our ordinary ways of checking things. Accordingly I have said nothing about the details of scientific validation, insisting only on its social character. Moreover, although I want to make a similar claim about other branches of systematic enquiry such as history and mathematics, each is conducted in accordance with its own tradition with its own special character and in order to be understood each requires separate and detailed study.

5. *Knowledge of what is social*

So far I have argued that much of human knowledge is social in the sense that it is acquired from and therefore shared with others, and that knowledge which is the product of systematic enquiry must be shared with others since it is not accepted as knowledge until it is validated inter-personally. I want now to draw attention to a further kind of knowledge which, since it is knowledge *of* what is social, must be acquired from others who already possess it. Knowledge of this sort is therefore doubly social. Examples of knowledge the content of which is social in this sense include knowledge of social traditions, including both practical traditions such as art and teaching and traditions of enquiry such as science and history, knowledge of social roles and knowledge of natural languages such as English or French.

Earlier it was pointed out that science may be thought of as a social activity carried on in accordance with a tradition, the purpose of which is to understand and explain the physical nature of the world we live in. It therefore provides a way of seeing according to which the world is partly intelligible, since some scientific progress has been made, and partly puzzling, since there are still many things which scientists do not understand. There is therefore a moving frontier of knowledge which the scientist is seeking to extend. It was, however, argued that nothing counts as scientific knowledge until it has been checked and accepted by the scientific community and therefore that knowledge of the present state of scientific progress can be obtained only from other scientists, since it is knowledge of what others know. That knowledge itself is still knowledge of the physical world, since that is what science is about. However, in checking a claim to have made a scientific discovery, others will want to know not only what was discovered but also how it was discovered. (What is important is not so much how a hypothesis or conjecture is generated but how it is tested experimentally.) This is partly because a tradition of enquiry lays down not only what is to be enquired into but also how such enquiries are to be conducted. Unless the proper methodology has been followed, the claim to knowledge will be rejected. Knowledge of the method employed also allows others to check the results of the enquiry, and in doing so they too must follow the prescribed procedures. In order to take part in the practice of science a scientist therefore needs to know what those procedures are, and that knowledge can only be obtained from existing practitioners. Moreover, it is social not only in its source but also in its content, since it is concerned not directly with the physical world but with the rules which scientists must follow in making their enquiries into that world. It is therefore knowledge of conventional rules of conduct. It follows that systematic knowledge of what is not social, the physical world, presupposes knowledge of what is social, the conventions and standards which govern scientific enquiry.

What is true of science is true also of other traditions, both practical and theoretical. It is true also of the ways of seeing and doing which are characteristic of a community as a whole. The human infant has to learn to become a member of such a community by learning how to behave and think like other members of the community and, as pointed out in Chapter 1, the way we see the world is closely connected with the language we use to describe it. As the quotation from Sapir put it, human beings are 'very much at the mercy of the particular language which has become the medium of expression for their society. We see and hear and otherwise experience the world as we do because the language habits of our community predispose certain choices of interpretation.' Language itself is a social institution which depends on linguistic conventions for the use and combination of words. Knowledge of these linguistic conventions can be learnt only from others since, like all other social phenomena, conventions exist only in being seen as what they are. They exist therefore only because they are seen as binding on those to whom they apply. The ancient king who raised a child in complete isolation in order to prove that the natural language of mankind was Hebrew was therefore bound to be disappointed. The unfortunate child grew up being unable to speak any language at all because there was no one from whom he could have learnt to do so.

6. Knowledge and teaching
It was pointed out in section III that all learning is learning by experience and consequently cannot take place unless the learner is in a position to have the relevant experience. In

general it is the learner's situation which provides that experience and, through that experience, the content of learning.
It is possible, however, to learn indirectly from others rather
than from what Descartes called 'the great book of the world',
and such learning is greatly facilitated by the development of
language. This in turn makes possible the growth of a shared
stock of common sense knowledge which is handed down from
one generation to the next. It may also lead to the establishment
of traditions of enquiry, such as science, history, philosophy and
mathematics, which allow nothing to count as knowledge unless
it has been inter-personally validated. Knowledge of what is
accepted as, for example, scientific knowledge, can be acquired
only from others. It could not possibly be acquired through the
learner's own direct experience. This is true also of knowledge of
the procedures laid down by the various traditions of enquiry for
checking claims to truth and, more generally, of knowledge of
linguistic conventions.

Contrary to the epistemological individualism of both Locke
and Descartes there are many things which can be learnt only
from somebody else who already knows them. The only way to
find out that the English for a dog or horseradish sauce is 'dog' or
'horseradish sauce', respectively, is from somebody who already
knows; it cannot be discovered by an examination of a dog or
horseradish sauce, however thorough.

In order to learn from others it is necessary to come into
contact with them. In a small community that contact may
occur as part of the normal course of social interaction
connected with eating, sharing accommodation, preparing
meals and other daily routines; children learn about livestock
and farming by helping with the work, and so on. As the
community becomes larger and more complex it becomes
increasingly necessary to make special arrangements to ensure
that young people have the opportunity to learn what they can
learn only from others. Such arrangements may take the form of
an apprenticeship system, as in the studios of the great Italian
Renaissance painters, or a social activity of teaching in which
teachers accept responsibility for the learning of others. The
need for the teacher to indicate to the learner what is to be learnt
is therefore a consequence of the social nature of knowledge
rather than a logical feature of teaching as such.

CHAPTER 7. EDUCATION, PERSONS AND SOCIETY

I. EDUCATION

1. The overall purpose of teaching

The approach to the philosophy of education adopted in Chapter 1 took the idea of teaching rather than that of education as its central concern, and teaching in turn was thought of as a social practice carried on by teachers in accordance with a social tradition. A tradition provides those engaged in a social practice with a way of seeing and doing which lays down how that practice is to be carried out. It does so by providing an overall purpose which tells them what to do and by providing the knowledge and skills which make it possible for them to do it. Attention has been drawn to many sorts of social practice besides teaching, including painting and medicine, and to theoretical enquiries such as science and history, which vary from one another in seeing things from a separate point of view and having a different overall purpose. It is the overall purpose of a practice which provides its principle of unity, allowing otherwise unconnected actions, for example all of the very varied things which teachers do, to be seen as part of the same practice. This is possible because what a person is doing may be described either from a very limited perspective or from a broader point of view. For example, what Polly is doing may be described either as putting the kettle on or as making a cup of tea; similarly when she warms the pot, puts the tea in and pours the boiling water on it she is also making a cup of tea. Thus actions which from a limited perspective are different become part of the same action when viewed from a broader point of view. In the same way, teachers do many different things in order to help others to learn; for example, they may show children how to hold a pencil, how to form letters and arrange them in words and so on in order to help them to learn to write. They also do many other things in order to help children to become educated; for example, they teach them to read, to perform arithmetical computations, to speak French or German, to appreciate literature and music and so on. In doing these things, which are also very different from each other, they are at the same time doing the same thing, which is helping others to become educated.

Different social practices are thus distinguished from one another, in the final analysis, by their overall purpose. The aim of some of them, including teaching and medicine, is practical, in the sense that it is to bring about change of one kind or another. The aim of others, such as science and history, is theoretical, in the sense that it is to discover the truth about one thing or another; science was therefore described as a systematic enquiry in the previous chapter. The aim of teaching is that of helping others to become educated, just as the aim of medicine is that of helping the sick. It is in this way that teaching is connected with education, as promised in the first chapter, and attention finally drawn to the children who are to be educated and who are consequently the objects of the teacher's concern. Once that has been done, there are grounds for referring to teaching – that is, the practice of teaching as well as what that practice aims to provide – as education, which will be done, as convenient, from here on. When the word 'education' is used in this sense the phrases 'becoming a teacher' and 'going into education' become synonymous, as do 'teaching' and 'educating'. This usage depends on the primary occurrence of the word education in the definition of the overall purpose of the practice of teaching, that of helping others to become educated.

2. Formal and informal education

It has been argued that teaching is a social practice, the overall purpose of which is that of helping others to become educated. The idea of education has been introduced only in order to describe, in a very general way, the overall purpose of teaching, although once that has been done there is no reason why the activity of teaching should not be referred to as the process of education or simply as education.

It might be objected that this way of putting things takes account only of what might be called formal education – that is, the education that takes place in educational institutions such as schools, colleges and universities – but fails to take account of the informal education which takes place outside such institutions. But it is widely agreed that at least part of a child's education is acquired informally, for example through contact with parents and other children and through direct experience of the world along the lines which Locke suggests. Secondly, it is clearly possible for there to be simple communities in which no provision is made for formal education and whose members do not include teachers who accept responsibility for the learning of others. Nevertheless it might be claimed that people in such communities do become educated, especially if it is accepted that to become educated is to learn to be a person.

It will be convenient to deal with the second objection first. The idea of education was introduced only in order to describe, in a very general way, a particular human purpose, the purpose shared by teachers. A society in which no one had that purpose would also be one in which no one had a use for the idea of education, so that no one in such a society would be in a position to describe anyone as either educated or uneducated. Its members might well distinguish between children and adults – indeed it is difficult to see how they could avoid doing so – and make various distinctions, including distinctions based on knowledge and wisdom, between one adult and another, but they could not make use of the idea of education in order to conceptualise such distinctions. In that sense there would be no such thing as education in that society. But its members would nevertheless have to learn to become persons and, in so far as to become educated is to learn to be a person, would in fact become educated. Lacking the idea of education, they would not be able to describe themselves as educated but we, who do possess that idea, would be able to do so.

The first objection – that the proposed definition of education fails to take account of informal education – can now be dealt with in a similar way. It is possible to speak of informal education because at least part of the results which teachers set out to achieve systematically may occur in the absence of their efforts. Indeed it is possible that in some instances teachers may

do more harm than good, just as a man trying to stop a shed
from falling down may cause it to do so through his well-
meaning but incompetent efforts. A comparison with farming
may be helpful here. Farming, like teaching, is a practical
activity, the overall point of which is to grow food and other
useful materials. It is possible, however, to obtain food and
materials from the land without farming it, for example by
picking fruit, gathering nuts, cutting reeds for thatching and so
on, and if these things were easily available in sufficient
quantities there would be no point in farming. It is therefore
possible that the things which are normally produced by
farming might be available in its absence, and if so we could
then speak of informal farming if we wished. Of course in order
to produce food in quantity, the farmer has to make use of
special techniques of cultivation and to grow specially bred
varieties of plant, so that what is produced on the farm may
differ considerably from its nearest wild equivalent: cultivated
strawberries, for example, may be dull and flat compared with
wild ones. It is also true that greedy or incompetent farming
may destroy or disfigure the countryside. But, whether we like it
or not, there has to be farming if the large numbers of people
who are alive today are to be fed. It may be the case that
something of this sort also applies in the case of education. It is
no part of my argument that teachers and schools are beyond
criticism, only that the idea of education derives from and does
not precede that of teaching. In short, we can speak of informal
education only because we also speak of formal education. In
the same way, we can speak of works of art (as opposed, for
example, to paintings) only because we have museums and art
galleries. Once having got the notion of a work of art we can
then think of things outside art galleries, such as the carvings on
Christmas Island, as works of art, even although those who
produced them could not.

3. Education, socialisation and values

A sharp contrast is often drawn between education and
socialisation. I agree that there is a contrast to be drawn,
although I do not think it is as sharp as is sometimes suggested.
The view that education and socialisation are very different
kinds of things arises partly out of the feeling that to have

become educated is to have achieved something of value, whereas socialisation is simply the process whereby impersonal social forces mould the personalities of individuals. To say that someone has become socialised is therefore to be noncommittal as to whether or not they have acquired anything of value. Those who speak in this way admit that the word education is sometimes used in a purely descriptive way to refer to what counts as becoming educated in societies other than our own. Used in this 'inverted commas' sense, as it is sometimes called, the word education loses its value connotation, so that it becomes possible to disapprove of education in Nazi Germany, for example, without contradiction. Similarly, it is possible to use the word education in a purely descriptive way to refer with disapproval to the products of the educational system of our own society so that, according to this usage to be educated is not necessarily a good thing.

That there is a connection between education and what is of value also follows from the view that the overall purpose of teaching is that somebody should become educated. If there is to be such a practice then somebody – either those engaged in the practice or those on behalf of whom they engage in it – must have that purpose as their own. They must see the goal to which it points as something worth striving for and as something for which it is worth making effort and sacrifices. This indeed was the point Flew relied on in the previous chapter; if somebody really has a purpose then it must matter to him whether he is achieving it. (It was, however, argued that it does not follow, as Flew claims, that he will take steps to find out whether he is achieving it.) More generally, to want something is to see it as having value, if only from your own point of view. Those who take part in a shared activity or live in the same society see things as having value not only from their own personal point of view but also from the point of view of the group to which they belong. To be a member of such a group is not only to share and to be expected to share the values of the group but to be required to do so, so that any shortcoming in this respect is regarded as a proper ground for criticism. Personal values are thus transformed into social values and given objectivity through being both shared and seen as shared. This makes it possible to draw a contrast between what a particular individual happens to value (that is, what is subjectively valued) and what he and others see as having objective value.

There are therefore two points of view from which education can be seen, the internal point of view of those whose commitment to the idea of education brings the activity of education into existence and provides it with its own internal dynamic, and the external point of view of those not so committed. From the first point of view, education cannot but be of value, but from the second point of view the question of its value is left open. Obviously we all adopt the second point of view when speaking of education in a society other than our own and some people adopt it when speaking of education in their own society.

If the term socialisation is confined to impersonal forces which are not informed by purpose, the value of the changes which it brings about can always be questioned. It cannot be assumed that they will be welcomed by those who intended to bring them about, since no one intended to do so. In contrast to education the term socialisation is neutral as to the value of the changes which it brings about but it does not follow that members of a particular society will themselves look on those changes in a neutral way, since the changes concerned include changes in their own attitudes and values and were brought about, if only haphazardly, through contact with other members of that society who already possessed them. Within a society there is bound to be a favourable attitude towards at least many of the changes brought about by socialisation. For example, in England we think that it is a good thing that children learn to speak English, even though they normally do so without any formal instruction and without it being necessary for anyone to actually decide that they should, although not of course without contact with people who themselves possess and value the ability to talk. It is not surprising therefore that when a child fails to learn to talk in the normal course of events it is considered important that special educational provision be made to help him to do so.

Thus although there is a distinction to be made between education (i.e. the activity of teaching) and socialisation, the distinction is not as sharp as sometimes suggested. In the case of education, we have already made up our minds about the value of the changes which it is intended to bring about; if we had not done so, then there would be no point in going to the trouble of bringing them about. Since the changes brought about by socialisation are not brought about intentionally, on the other hand, there is always scope for us to reflect on them and decide whether we approve or disapprove of them. But we are likely to approve of most of them, since they are the principal source of our standards of judgement, and if we approve of them we may well wish to speak of informal education.

4. Becoming educated

It is the overall purpose of a social practice which provides it with its principle of unity and makes it the kind of practice which it is. The overall purpose of teaching, it has been suggested, is that of helping others to become educated. What then is it to become educated?

This question can be understood in two very different ways.[1] It can be understood either as a question asked in the context of and about a particular educational practice and its traditions, or it can be understood as a question about what makes a social practice an *educational* rather than, say, a medical or religious one. When it is understood in the first way, the answer provided may take the form of a description in general terms of the aims of that practice and their history, especially of the changing ideas in terms of which it has been conceptualised, or it may take the form of a prescription for its future development. Both kinds of answer may be combined in a philosophy of education of the kind described in section I of Chapter 3, the answer actually given depending on the particular practice about which it is asked. When the question is understood in the second way, however, what is required is a philosophical account of the principle of identity according to which we recognise different educational practices and traditions as examples of the same kind of thing in being educational rather than medical or religious. It is this more general question which I wish to answer by suggesting that to become educated is to learn to be a person.

If to become educated, in general, is to learn to be a person, then to become educated in a particular society is also to learn to be a person. And, just as 'becoming educated' can be understood in two different ways, so also can 'person'. Understood in the first way, the members of any recognisably human society must be persons; understood in the second way, what counts as a person is laid down by the society concerned. An account of the concept of a person understood in the first way would be philosophical and descriptive, whereas an account of the concept of a person in the second sense would be prescriptive, at least for members of that society. Correspondingly, each educational tradition has its own ideal concept of what a person ought to be which provides the final point of reference for the educational practice which it guides, and which may be spelt out in a philosophy of education of the kind discussed in section I of Chapter 3. It is with the first philosophical account of a person that I will be concerned in the next section.

II. THE CONCEPT OF A PERSON

1. Assessment of Locke's view of a person

I have suggested that to become educated is to learn to be a person. The plausibility of that suggestion depends on the account given of the concepts of learning and of a person. Learning was discussed in section III of Chapter 6 and will not be considered again here. A great deal has also been said about the concept of a person at different places in previous chapters, including Chapter 2. Locke begins his *Essay*, in fact, by pointing out that 'it is the *understanding* that sets man above the rest of sensible beings, and gives him all the advantage and dominion which he has over them'.[2] By the understanding he means the ability to acquire ideas and therefore to think and acquire beliefs and knowledge. Locke's basic assumption therefore is that a person is a sensible being (that is, an animal) that thinks.

It might be helpful to recall some of the main points in Locke's account and the criticisms of them in Chapter 2. What makes it possible for us to think, according to Locke, is the fact that we can acquire ideas of things through our experience of them, so that our ideas are produced, straightforwardly, by the things of which they are ideas. Each person therefore constructs his own picture of the world through his personal contact with it, although since the world is the same for everybody, one person's picture of it is much the same as anyone else's. It was argued, however, that the way we see and, more generally, think about things depends on a way of seeing which can be acquired only by a process of learning from others who already possess it, being passed from one generation to the next, from that to the next, and so on. A way of seeing is thus the work of many generations, not that of an individual working on his own. It can be more easily passed on in this way because of the fact that persons express their thoughts in language, making it possible for them to be communicated to others. Indeed a natural language, which in the nature of the case is a shared possession, is itself an objective repository of a way of thinking. As far as behaviour is concerned, also, Locke thinks of each person as a rational individualist, deciding for himself what to do on the basis of his own wishes and in the light of his own capabilities. It was argued, however, that a way of seeing is also a way of doing and that we behave in the way we do for the most part because we have learnt to do so from other members of the society to which we belong.

None of these criticisms affects Locke's basic assumption that a person is an animal that thinks. They are directed only at his account of what it is to think, which is atomistic and individualistic. Some such account might be adequate for the thought of a Robinson Crusoe who, abandoned in infancy on a desert island, nevertheless managed to survive and grow to manhood. Such a man would not, however, 'be set above the rest of sensible beings', as Locke puts it; he would live a life which differed little in its broad outline from that of any other large intelligent mammal. He would make only those distinctions in his thinking which were suggested to him by his personal experience and perceived needs and engage only in those projects which his own ingenuity could suggest. Although we can only speculate, it seems unlikely that it would occur to him to build himself a shelter, for example, or to use tools or store food, and it seems highly unlikely that he would learn to use fire to keep himself warm or to cook his food, to domesticate animals or grow food, or to make clothes for himself. Moreover, even if we suppose that an infant girl, Emily, was also abandoned on the island at the same time, and that in due course she and Robinson had children, and that their children had children, and so on for many generations, it would at best be a very long time before a recognisably human way of life started to emerge. We do know, however, that there is at least a chance that it would do so, because we know that this is in fact what has happened elsewhere. What sets man above the rest of sensible beings, then, is not simply the fact that he thinks, but that he thinks in accordance with a way of thinking which is both the product of and shared with many others, and that, as a result, he not only lives in and is able to think about the physical world but also lives in and is able to think about a social world which, in a real sense, is brought into being by that way of thinking.

2. *Persons as having a conception of the physical world*
Whenever we think, we must think about something; it is its content – that is, what it is about – that makes a thought the thought which it is. What we can think about depends for its detail on the particular concepts at our disposal; for example, we can think about cats or cathode ray tubes only if we possess the concept of a cat or of a cathode ray tube. And the concepts at our disposal depend, in turn, on the way of thinking, or conceptual scheme as I will now call it, which we have acquired as a result of growing up and becoming educated in the particular society to which we happen to belong. But although conceptual schemes differ in their detail, something can be said about the most general features which they all share. Very generally, what we think about is the world we live in – what is sometimes called the external world or, as Locke puts it, the reality of things – and ourselves, and what makes it possible for us to think about them is our possession of the concepts of a physical object and of a person. It is our possession of these concepts which, more than any others, gives structure to our thought. To be a person is therefore to possess a conceptual scheme which includes, as its most general features, the concepts of a physical object and of a person. I will say something about each of these in turn.

When we think about a physical object such as a table or a chair we think of it as spatio-temporally extended and consequently as uniquely located in a spatio-temporal framework of three spatial and one temporal dimension. We think of it, that is, as having some endurance through time and as being located somewhere throughout that period of time. As persons, however, we ourselves possess bodies which are themselves physical objects, thus we also must be located somewhere throughout the period of our existence. It follows that we may be in the same place as a physical object and consequently in a position to find out and form beliefs about it through the use of our senses. On the other hand, since sense perception depends on causal interaction between our sense organs and what is seen, we cannot see objects *unless* we are at the same place as them. But it is part of our conception of physical reality that the existence of physical objects is independent of our perception of them. We do not suppose, that is, that they do not exist simply because we cannot see them or that they exist only as long as we can see them. To see a physical object such as a table or a chair as here now is at the same time to think of it as having been in existence prior to our perception of it and, other things being equal, as continuing to exist when we can no longer see it. To possess a concept of physical objects as spatio-temporally extended therefore is *ipso facto* to possess a spatio-temporal point of view which allows us to think about and see ourselves as located in a world which extends indefinitely beyond that small fragment of it which lies within the range of our senses at any one moment. There is a world out there, beyond the here and now of our present experience, which we think of as existing independently of our perception of it. We already know some things about it and can learn more by moving about and by observing the unfolding of events in it with the passage of time.

It may be helpful to illustrate this very abstract account by telling a simple story about an ordinary sort of person called Fred. At time $t1$ at place $p1$ Fred, at home after a hard day's work, looks around in an enquiring sort of way and sees a so-and-so; 'ah', he says to himself, 'there is a so-and-so here now'. A little later, at time $t2$, Fred has moved on and is now at his favourite pub, The P2 Arms, at $p2$. But although he is now surrounded by the warmth and comfort he knows so well, he cannot get the so-and-so out of his mind. 'The so-and-so was there then – at $p1$ at $t1$ – so I suppose it will still be there now – that is, at $p1$ at $t2$. And I suppose that unless someone has moved it it will still be there when I get back from the pub.' Time passes, closing time is called, and Fred returns home to his house at $p1$. 'Yes, I thought so', he says to himself, 'the so-and-so is still here. And what's more I expect the so-and-so thing will still be here in the morning'; and off he goes to bed. In this story Fred begins by identifying a so-and-so *as* a so-and-so; he is able to do so because he possesses the concept of a so-and-so and because there is a so-and-so sensibly present at that place, $p1$, at that time, $t1$. Later, at the pub, he is able to think about the so-and-so, even although it is not sensibly present at that place, $p2$, at that time, $t2$. Indeed, he does not think of it as at $p2$ at $t2$; he thinks of it first as at $p1$ at $t1$ and then as at $p1$ at $t3$. And when he returns home at $p1$ at $t3$, he not only identifies the so-and-so which, as he expected, is still there, *as* a so-and-so but also reidentifies it as the very same so-and-so which was here then, that is, at $p1$ at $t1$. Thus the possession of a conceptual scheme which included concepts of physical objects such as that of a so-and-so brought with it a spatio-temporal point of view which allowed Fred to think not only about the here and now but also about things at other places and other times, both past and future. The possession of a conceptual scheme thus liberates a person from the here and now and allows him to live his life in a world which is extended in both space and time and so to live a much fuller and richer life than would otherwise be possible. Let us suppose, by way of contrast, that Fred has a ferret which lives in a cage under the kitchen sink and which does not possess a conceptual scheme or therefore a spatio-temporal point of view. The ferret can be aware only of those things which are, from time to time, now present in its immediate surroundings, although of course it cannot be aware of them as physical objects, since it does not possess any concepts of physical objects and, if it can be said to think of all, it can think only about what is here now, since it does not possess a spatio-temporal point of view. It cannot, for example, think with pleasure today of the joy it experienced yesterday in getting its teeth into Fred's finger.

The possession of a conceptual scheme allows a person not only to form beliefs but also to formulate and pursue purposes. The behaviour of all animals which are capable of movement is directed towards goals which, if achieved, place them in a better poisition to survive and flourish. For the most part we suppose that their behaviour is directly controlled by external stimuli; we do not therefore credit them with any insight into the ends served by their behaviour or suppose that they think up and follow plans in order to achieve them. Persons, on the other hand, are aware of their situation and of the possibilities for change inherent in it, and when they act in order to change it they have some insight into the ends towards which their behaviour is directed and the way in which they need to behave in order to achieve them. Through possessing a spatio-temporal point of view persons can not only look forward to a future which will be revealed by the passage of time but also towards a future which is to some extent of their own making.[3]

This further development in the account of what is involved in the possession of a conceptual scheme can also be illustrated by reconsidering the story about Fred. At $t1$ at $p1$, it will be recalled, Fred was at home having his tea but his thoughts were elsewhere, at the P2 Arms at $p2$; indeed, he was looking forward to the time when, at $t2$, he would be able to join them. He was able to anticipate his presence there because he had already formed the intention of going there. Accordingly, shortly after $t1$, he put on his cap and muffler, said goodbye to his ferret, and set off in the direction of the P2 Arms. His presence there at $t2$ was therefore no accident; he knew before he set out where he wanted to go, why he wanted to go there and how to get there.

3. *Persons as having a conception of a social world*

To be a person, it has been suggested, is to possess a conceptual scheme which includes as its most general features the concept of a physical object and the concept of a person. Something has been said about the difference which the possession of the concept of a physical object makes to a person in allowing him to form a picture of a physical world which extends beyond his own immediate situation and to change the world in ways which are foreseen and intended through his own efforts. Something must now be said about the differences which the possession of the concept of a person makes. I will begin by comparing the position of a physical object, an animal which possesses the concept of a physical object, and a person who possesses the concept of a person.

To possess a concept of any kind is to possess the ability to see (or more generally to think about) things of a kind as being of that kind; for example, to possess the concept of a table or a cat is to possess the ability to see tables as tables and cats as cats. If a table possessed the concept of a table, therefore, it would not only be able to see other tables as tables but also, since it is itself a table, to see itself as a table. Since, of course, tables do not possess any concepts, this does not happen. It draws attention, however, to an important distinction between the *application* of a concept and its *ascription*. We are happy to *apply* the concept of a table to a table, since to do so is simply to see it as a table, but it would be absurd to *ascribe* that or any other concept to it. However, we might be prepared to allow that cats have their own feline view of the world and to ascribe concepts of physical objects such as that of a table to them. It does not follow that we would also be prepared to ascribe the concept of a cat to them, which would be to see them as seeing themselves and each other as having such a view. Indeed it was assumed in section I of Chapter 4 that we would not do so. In that section it was supposed that a cat might be regarded as causally responsible, or responsible as agent, for killing a canary, for example, but that we would not on that account regard it as socially responsible or accountable for what it had done. We would not do so because, although we were prepared to *apply* the concept of an agent to the cat, we were not prepared to *ascribe* it. The cat was an agent but was not aware of itself as an agent and therefore was not in a position to assess its actions or to suppose that it might have acted differently. Moreover, since it did not see itself as itself at any one time, it could not see itself as the *same* individual (cat or person) at different times. It could not therefore connect any punishment or blame it might receive at a later time with its own earlier action in killing the canary. In short, although it was an agent it could not be regarded as a responsible agent.

Although unwilling to admit that a cat could see itself as itself and as the same individual at different times, we might nevertheless be prepared to admit that a solitary Robinson Crusoe, supposed in subsection 1 above to have been abandoned at birth on a desert island, might come to do so. After all, for Locke the idea of a person is presumably either a simple idea of reflection or a complex of such ideas, and Locke's own formal definition of a person is that of 'a thinking intelligent being that has reason and reflection and can consider itself as itself, the same thinking thing in different times and places'.[4] If so then

Crusoe might well come to criticise some of his own earlier actions, such as that of killing all the giant tortoises on the island, as imprudent. But as long as he remained alone there could be no possibility of his actions being criticised by reference to impersonal standards, either by himself or anybody else. Only the introduction of Emily and, in due course, her children into the story makes it possible to see how such standards might emerge. Given both his possession of the concept of a person and the actual presence of other people, Crusoe would then be in a position not only to see himself as a person but also to see other persons as persons. He could then go on to see others as seeing him as a person, to see others seeing him as seeing them as persons, and so on; similarly, the other persons concerned would be in a position to see him in the same way. To use the term introduced earlier, it would be possible for relations of reciprocal self-awareness to develop between all of the persons on the island, which in turn would make the emergence of impersonal standards possible. It would also allow the development of social roles, perhaps initially closely connected with biological function, each with its own objectively defined rights and duties.

In order to see how this might happen, a distinction must be made between impersonal standards (or social rules) and group habits. Even if alone on the island, Crusoe could be expected to develop certain habitual ways of behaving, such as using cupped hands in order to drink rather than drinking directly from a stream, and if there were a number of people on the island many of them could be expected to behave in the same way. Indeed, something like this presumably happened in the colony of Japanese macaque monkeys discussed in the previous chapter; once one monkey had learnt how to separate rice from sand by throwing it into the sea, others followed its example. A group habit, then, is simply an habitual way of behaving which most members of a group happen to share. An individual who did not wish to conform to such a habit (for example a monkey which did not like the taste of salt water) would be under no pressure to do so. But if it is assumed that the members of the Crusoe family came to possess reciprocal self-awareness, it would be possible for them to come to regard some of those ways of behaving as impersonal standards which all were required to obey whether they wished to do so or not. A person who accepted such a standard would then not only see himself as obliged to behave in the required way but would also see others as under a similar obligation, and, conversely, would see others as seeing him in the same way. For those who accepted it the standard would not only give them a reason for behaving in the required way themselves but would also provide them with grounds for criticising those who failed to conform. The standard would then have been brought into existence through its recognition as a standard by the majority of the members of the group for whom it functioned in that way.

The possession of the concept of a person makes it possible for an individual to be seen and to see himself as socially responsible or accountable for his actions; it also makes it possible for a group of such persons to acquire impersonal standards by reference to which such actions can be judged. Standards which apply to all members of a community, thus giving it its basic identity, and which are thought of as having overriding importance, are usually called moral standards. They give shape and purpose both to the lives of individuals and to the community in which those lives are lived, laying down a point of view – the moral point of view of the community – about how life is to be lived in that community. Standards which apply only to those engaged in a particular practical activity such as painting or teaching, or in a theoretical activity such as science or history, have been described in earlier chapters as the ways of doing provided by a tradition. Part of learning to be a person is therefore learning to be a moral agent in a moral community, most members of which are also moral agents. This is a conclusion which is consistent with the insight, which goes back to Plato, that moral education is an essential and central part of education. Similarly, a further part of learning to be a person is learning to take part in the various theoretical and practical activities of the community and to occupy social roles such as that of a teacher.

4. Communication

In subsection 2 it was argued that the possession of the concept of a physical object not only allows its possessor to form a picture of an objectively existing world but also brings with it a spatio-temporal point of view from which to survey that world. In subsection 3 it was argued that the possession of the concept of a person allows persons to see themselves not only as persons but also as responsible persons living in a community of such persons. It was also suggested that persons can see themselves as members of a community only if relations of reciprocal self-awareness develop between them, making it possible for impersonal standards of behaviour to emerge.

Reciprocal self-awareness makes possible a further development, that of communication, especially through the use of language, which is especially important from the point of view of teaching. It was pointed out in section III of the previous chapter that although sense experience is important in informing a person about his own immediate situation, most of a person's knowledge is acquired only indirectly from other people. This is true not only of common sense knowledge but also, more importantly, of the products of systematic enquiries such as science, mathematics and history. Indeed it was pointed out that nothing counts as, for example, scientific knowledge unless it has been checked and accepted by the recognised authorities in the relevant area. Its content must therefore be communicated to them in order to make this possible. It was also argued that knowledge of what is social can be acquired only from others who already possess it. This includes not only knowledge of the conventions which regulate scientific and other branches of enquiry but also knowledge of social roles and moral rules. Thus the knowledge which systematic enquiry makes possible and the possibility of an orderly life in a community governed by impersonal standards of behaviour both depend on communication, and it will be argued that this in turn depends on the existence of relations of reciprocal self-awareness between the parties to it. The idea of communication is thus important for an understanding of a specifically human way of life and especially for an understanding of the contribution which the social practice of teaching makes to such a way of life.

Communication may be initially defined as the transmission of information, and the transmission of information involves a source, a channel along which the information is transmitted, and a receiver. The telephone engineers of the Bell Telephone company, with whom this communication theory approach originated, were primarily interested in the channel along which information is transmitted. In particular they were interested in the amount of information which it could carry, since this is always limited, and the extent to which information was lost or distorted in transmission, since no channel is one hundred per cent efficient. It is easy to see why these questions were important to the American army, for whom the company supplied field telephones, and indeed to anyone developing a commercial telephone system. But the conceptual framework which this approach offers has been found helpful in a wide variety of contexts. Three examples of things which can be thought of in this way will be given. I will then go on to consider what needs to be added in order to arrive at an understanding of communication between persons, for example between a teacher and a pupil.

First, light now reaching the earth from distant parts of the universe comes from stars which ceased to exist when the universe was still very new. It might therefore be said that information about the origin of the universe is being transmitted from those stars to the earth. Secondly, it is possible to think about perception in the same sort of way. When we see things and thus acquire ideas of them, Locke tells us, 'it is evident some singly imperceptible bodies must come from them to the eyes, and thereby convey to the brain some *motion*, which produces these *ideas* which we have of them in us'.[5] Locke is in effect saying here that perception can be thought of as the transmission of information from an external object along a channel consisting of 'imperceptible bodies' to a receptor. Thirdly, in some cases perceptual information may originate with another animal rather than with an external object as such. An example given in section III, 3 of the previous chapter was that of the mother blackbird which emitted a warning cry, to which her chicks responded by crouching.

Although these examples conform to the original definition of communication, in varying degrees they lack certain features which communication between persons could be expected to have. First, we would expect that a person who had received information about the origin of the universe, for example, would have learnt something and would expect the learning concerned to be cognitive. (Cognitive learning was defined in section III, 3 of the previous chapter as learning which results in the formation and modification of beliefs.) Therefore we would expect a person who had received information to have acquired beliefs of one sort or another. Returning to the first example, however, the earth cannot be said to have learnt anything since, being neither an animal or a person, it is incapable of learning. (A scientist might learn about the origin of the universe from a study of the light reaching the earth, but that is another matter.) In the third example, the blackbird chicks could be said to have learnt about the presence of danger but only in the sense that they responded adaptively to their mother's cry. They did not receive information in the sense of acquiring beliefs. However, the second example, that of perception, passes this test; seeing, in general, is believing, at least for creatures capable of belief.

Secondly, in human communication we would expect the person who was the source of the information to intend to convey that information to the recipient. In the first example, the ancient stars clearly did not intend to inform the earth about the origin of the universe. Similarly, when we see something such as a chair, the chair does not intend to tell us about itself. What we say about the third example will depend on whether we are prepared to credit blackbirds with beliefs and intentions. It was assumed in the previous chapter that we would not be prepared to do so, and if that is correct then we cannot say that the mother bird intended to inform her chicks about the presence of danger. Therefore none of the examples pass this test. Before proceeding let us consider a further example which would pass it, that of Fred who says to his brother Billy: 'That ferret is a vicious brute.' In this example Fred obviously intends Billy to acquire the belief that the ferret is a vicious brute, so that the requirement that both belief and intention be involved in communication is met.

Thirdly, a further important feature of human communication is that the belief should be conveyed through the use of symbols. It could be argued indeed that it is the use of symbols which makes belief and more generally, thought, possible in the first place. Locke, for example, claims that it is the possession of ideas which makes it possible for us to think, and if ideas are construed as mental images this is very plausible. What Locke actually says, however, is that ideas are 'whatsoever is the object

of the understanding when a man thinks',[6] in other words that
ideas are what we think *about*. This is very misleading. When
Fred thinks that his ferret is a bit off colour, he is obviously
thinking about his ferret, which is in the cage under the sink, and
not about his idea of a ferret which is in his head. What Locke
should have said is that we *make use* of ideas in order to think
about what our ideas are ideas of, not that we think *about* ideas;
thus Fred is able to think about his ferret because he possesses an
idea of it. But whether belief as such depends on the use of
symbols is not immediately relevant. What is relevant is that the
communication of beliefs, in the sense of their intentional
conveyance, depends on their use. For if beliefs are to be
communicated they must be expressed in some way which
makes them available to others, and that can be done only
through the use of symbols which are publicly observable and
which must therefore be physical rather than mental. Ideas
could not be used for this purpose because they are mental and
therefore private to their possessors.

What then are symbols? In criticising Locke's view that ideas
are what we think about, it was taken for granted that a symbol
must be a symbol *of* something; it is because ideas are always
ideas *of* things that they can be regarded as symbols. Anyone
who discusses ideas cannot help confirming this, if only
unwittingly; whenever Locke, for example, refers to an idea he
does so by saying what it is an idea of – 'the idea of heat and cold,
light and darkness, white and black, motion and rest', for
example, and so on.[7] From the point of view of thought or the
communication of thought what is important about an idea – or
anything else which is used as a symbol – is what it is an idea or
symbol *of*; that is, what it is used to stand for or represent and
therefore what it allows us to think about or what thoughts it
allows us to communicate. There is, however, a further question
which can be asked about an idea or any other symbol; that is,
what is it in itself? It is natural to read Locke, for example, as
thinking of ideas as mental images but, as noted above, symbols
can be used to communicate only if they are physical and
therefore publicly observable. Anything which is physical,
however, can be used as a symbol, that is, used to stand for
something other than itself, and the choice of what is actually
used will depend only on convenience. Facial expressions,

gestures and vocalisations, perhaps in combination, are obvious choices but objects, such as flowers, can also be used. Whatever form a symbol takes it will always be possible to distinguish between what it is, for example a sound of such and such an intensity and pitch or a flower of a certain shape and colour, and what it stands for or means. A flower, for example, may be used to stand for affection.

A symbol such as a flower may be used by one person with the intention of communicating something to someone else. But suppose that Robinson Crusoe gave Emily a flower in order to tell her that he was fond of her. She would be able to see the flower, since flowers are publicly observable, but it does not follow that in doing so she would learn what Robinson Crusoe was trying to communicate to her. In order to do so she would have to know that the flower was being used *as* a symbol and what it was being used to symbolise; but she could not find that out simply by examining the flower. In itself, the flower would be no different from any of the other flowers growing on the island; it would differ only in the use which was made of it by Robinson Crusoe. In other words, a communication will be successful only if the person intended to receive it realises the intention with which the symbols which give it perceptible form are used. A communication can therefore be *expected* to be successful only if it is reasonable for the person making it to suppose that the person intended to receive it will in fact perceive the intention behind what is done in making it. The person intending to communicate must therefore have intended to bring about a change in belief in the person to whom the communication was addressed through their perception of his intention to do so.[8] In other words, communication is made possible only by reciprocal self-awareness between the parties to it, as claimed at the beginning of this discussion.

In the situation considered above – two people trying to communicate with each other in the absence of a shared *system* of communication – any success which they had would depend on their intimate knowledge of each other. But once communication was established conventional meanings would quickly become attached to symbols. For example, once Emily realised what Robinson Crusoe meant by the flower on the first occasion on which he used it, she would quickly realise what he meant by it on subsequent occasions; eventually she would come to see it as *having* that meaning without needing to discover what he intended it to mean on every occasion he used it. Indeed, a stage would be reached when she was in a position to correct his use of symbols, pointing out that he had misused them by breaking the normative rules which had become established between them for their use. There would, that is, be a transition from what a particular person meant by a symbol on a particular occasion to what the symbol meant, irrespective of who used it. In other words, as argued in section III, 3 of the previous chapter, communication allows the development of a shared, public language which permits communication, even between strangers, to take place easily and quickly. What needs to be added to communication are impersonal standards, similar to those discussed in 3 above, which lay down the use to which symbols, now more familiarly called words, are to be put and the ways in which they can be combined to allow new and more complex thoughts to be communicated. Given a shared knowledge of linguistic conventions, persons who wish to communicate with each other do not have to find out, on every occasion, the meaning which each attaches to the symbols which they are using. They already know their conventional meaning and now only need to pay attention to the content of what is said.

Finally, I would like to draw attention to the distinction between communicating a belief to people – that is, telling them – and putting them into a position to acquire that belief for themselves.[9] Fred used the words 'that ferret is a vicious brute', intending in doing so to get his brother to believe that this was the case, but he could have achieved the same result, that is, of getting his brother to believe that this was so, without actually telling him. For example, he could have taken him gently by the hand and stuck his finger in the ferret's cage, leaving the ferret to do the rest. In that case, he would have acted with the intention of getting Billy to acquire the belief but he would not have done so by telling him; he would simply have put him in a position to acquire the belief for himself. If he had happened to be a teacher who was a keen advocate of discovery methods, he may even have thought it better to get him to learn for himself rather than simply telling him. Any knowledge he gained would be based directly on his personal experience and would not depend on the

authority of an informant. It would also be more likely to be
remembered better and its implications more fully understood.
But it is easy to see that there would be advantages in telling him
instead, as Billy would certainly have told him. In any case, as
has already been stressed, there are many things, including
matters of educational importance, which the learner cannot
find out for himself and can acquire only from others. In this and
other ways, therefore, dependence on and trust in others is a
necessary part of the human condition.

5. *Education, persons and society*

So far in this section I have outlined an account of the concept of
a person according to which persons possess a conception of
themselves and of the world they live in. Their possession of a
conception of the physical world allows them to form a picture of
the physical world and, at the same time, to acquire a spatio-
temporal point of view from which to contemplate it; and this in
turn makes it possible for them to formulate and pursue plans for
changing it. Their possession of a conception of themselves
allows them to see themselves as agents and therefore to
understand their own responsibility for the changes which they
bring about. It also allows them not only to see themselves as
persons but to see themselves as seen as persons by others who
are also seen as seeing themselves in the same way. This in turn
makes possible the emergence of impersonal standards or social
rules for both behaviour and the use of words. Persons therefore
see themselves as living not only in a physical world but also in a
social world, or society, which is brought into being and defined
by those standards. They see themselves not simply as *in* but as
members of that world. They make it what it is but it in turn
makes them what they are, that is, persons who in being persons
are not simply individuals but members of a society.[10]

It follows from this account of the concept of a person that
there is a close connection between the concepts of education,
persons and society. To become educated, it has been suggested,
is to learn to be a person. To become a person, however, is to
become a member of a society. To become educated is therefore
to become a member of a society and so to have learnt what it is
to be and live as a member of that society. It follows that a
human infant abandoned on an otherwise deserted island could

become a person, if it survived at all, only in a very minimal
sense. Biologically it would be, and would remain, a member of
the same species as the rest of the human race. It would therefore
possess the same ability to think and learn as any other human
child but it would not have the opportunity to learn what other
children learn and consequently its life could be no more than
the life of any intelligent animal. A child brought up by apes, as
was Lord Greystoke's son and heir in Edgar Rice Burroughs'
story, would have the opportunity to learn whatever ways of
thinking and doing apes have and would to that extent be more
fortunate; but in so far as it became a person it would become a
person who was a member of an ape society rather than of a
human society. Indeed in all cases the kind of person a child
becomes depends on the particular society in which it grows up
and the place it comes to occupy in that society.

Although a society can exist, and continue to exist, only
through its members, it cannot be identified with the particular
persons who happen to be its members at any one moment of
time. A society continues as the same society from one
generation to the next. In the words of Edmund Burke, it is 'a
partnership not only between those who are living, but between
those who are living, those who are dead, and those who are to
be born'.[11] It has an identity and a character which is given not
simply for any one individual but also, for the most part, for any
one generation. New members are born into it and in due course
die; it survives their deaths since they in turn are replaced by
succeeding generations. The continuity of a society therefore has
a biological basis in the lives of its members. But although its
members are born into it, they can make no contribution to its
continuity until they acquire a social identity. They acquire
such an identity through interaction with their social environment, that is, with other people who already possess a social
identity, and so become part of that environment; they are then
themselves available to influence the generations which follow.
If a society is to survive therefore this process of social regener-
ation must continue without interruption. As pointed out in
section I, 2, in a simple society there is no need to make special
provision to ensure that this happens. The young learn how to
behave – how, that is, to behave as a member of the community
to which they belong – through informal contacts with their

elders. There is therefore no need to make special provision for their education but once division of labour is introduced and specialised knowledge and skills develop, it becomes increasingly necessary to do so. In a society as complex and sophisticated as our own, with its vigorous intellectual and cultural traditions, the development of educational institutions is inevitable.

There is thus a close connection between the concepts of education and society. It follows that there is a similar connection between education and youth such that, in general, it is the young who are educated and, during that process, learn to become persons. But although this seems obvious, it is a point which has been frequently denied or ignored. According to Professor Peters' influential account of the concept of education, outlined in Chapter 1, education is the process of passing on, or initiating persons into, things of value which, when they possess them, will enrich their lives. The sole aim or end of education is the enhancement of the lives of individuals as an end in itself, and to think of education as having a social function is to confuse education and socialisation. It follows from such an account that education can take place at any time during a person's life and, ideally, should continue throughout it. There is no special reason why it is the young who should be educated, although of course it is the normal practice and may have its advantages. If this view is correct it should make sense to suggest that the normal order of things – education in childhood, work in adulthood and leisure in old age – should be reversed, and that children should do what they wish while the old go to school.

The reason why it is in general the young who are educated is not simply an accident of chronology, like vulnerability to measles, but is rooted in the logic of the situation. What has to be acquired must be acquired from others – other members of the same society – and they have to acquire it themselves before they can make it available in turn. If the old rather than the young were educated there would therefore be a problem about who would educate the old. Perhaps they could educate each other, first being educated and then educating others, but this would depend on the reintroduction of a distinction between the young and the old, even if only between the young-old and the old-old. However, there is a more serious objection. As pointed out above, a society depends for its existence on the persons who are its members. Moreover, if the society is to maintain its identity, its members must be – indeed, must become – persons of the right kind. To interfere with the process of socialisation, and especially with that part of it which has become institutionalised in education, would be to change the character of the persons who are its members and therefore to change the character of the society itself. If what we now call education were deferred until old age the result would be a totally different society if, indeed, any viable society resulted. And we would still presumably wish to enquire, of such a society, by what formal or informal means its members acquired whatever social identity they possessed during the greater part of their lives. We would therefore have good reason to reintroduce a concept of education which connected education with the young.

It should now be clear that what is wrong with the Peters' view of education outlined above is not what it asserts but what it denies, the connection between education and society and between education and youth. Education is connected with youth because it is a process of becoming, a preparation for life which would be pointless in old age, since we can prepare only for what lies in the future and the old, by definition, have no future. It puts us in a position to live our lives in the society to which we belong, taking advantage of the opportunities which it offers for life and living. In doing so, however, it also provides that society with the kind of members it must have if it is to continue to exist and maintain its own identity and character. Education therefore has a social function, that of perpetuating the society of which it is a part, and it also has a personal function, that of preparing individuals for a place in the society. These are not alternatives, one of which can be fulfilled at the expense of the other, but two aspects of the same thing. It is certainly true, as the Peters' account suggests, that education is a benefit to the persons who receive it, but it is also true that it is at the same time a benefit to the society to which they belong.

The connection between education, persons and society means that education has a two-sided character in looking backward to the past of the society to which it belongs and looking forward to the future, both of that society and of the persons being educated. To say that education is backward looking is to say once again that it is a social practice carried on in accordance with a tradition and therefore looks to the past for its content and values. To say that education is forward looking is to say that it is a process of forming; the traditional metaphor of a potter and his clay is apt if not taken too literally. Education gives character and social identity to individuals who, initially, are no more than human animals in a social context and who have to *become* persons. In doing so it places them in a social tradition within which they can live their own lives and at the same time contribute to the stability and continuity of that tradition. Education therefore looks forward both to the lives which the persons becoming educated will live and to the future of the society in which they will live them.

The denial of the connection between education and society and between education and youth leads naturally to the view that education can and should continue throughout a person's life. This view seems plausible because we can never say that a person's education is complete in the way in which we can say that he has stopped growing, but it does not necessarily follow that a person's education cannot be said to have come to an end. Moreover, the view that education should continue throughout a person's life leads to the neglect of an important distinction, that between becoming something and being that thing. The potter who makes a vase out of clay does not go on making it forever just because, in some sense, it is never as good as it might be. He stops working on it when it is as good as he can make it or because he has spent as much time on it as he can afford and has to move on to something else. The making of the vase is then complete, even although it is less perfect than it might be, and it can be put to the use for which it was made. Being formed into a vase and being a vase are thus very different things; indeed, it is the latter which gives point to the former. Education is also a process of forming, although in this case the forming of persons. It is the idea of the initial giving of character or personality to persons and equipping them with what they will need in the way of knowledge and skills in order to live in and contribute to the society to which they belong. Becoming a person is in many ways different to becoming a vase, and the line between becoming and being a person is not as clear cut as that between becoming and being a vase. Nevertheless the distinction remains, and is essential for a proper understanding of the notion of education.

One reason why this distinction is easy to overlook is that, once formed, things may undergo further change. In some cases the changes concerned may be trivial or even harmful; for example, the clay of a vase may eventually become brittle or the glaze fade. Other changes, however, may constitute an improvement. A Christmas cake, for example, may improve with keeping. Similarly, persons may continue to learn and become fuller and richer as persons after their education has been completed. But it does not follow that these further changes can be conceptualised in terms of the notion of becoming educated. Other ways of doing so are available to us, such as becoming more mature, more experienced, wiser or better informed. The ways in which people change as they grow older are not always for the better; they may become set in their ways, lose interest in things they once valued, become indifferent and uncaring in their relations with others and so on but we do not need to conceptualise these changes in terms of the notion of education. Similarly, we do not say that old people who have become senile have become uneducated, even although what is lost in senility may be part of what was gained through education.

The distinction between the changes involved in becoming a person and those which take place after doing so is best illustrated by considering a particular social practice such as that of painting or teaching. The difference between being introduced to a tradition, such as that of European painting, and taking part in it and perhaps contributing to its development is obvious, even though it may be impossible to say exactly when the transition occurs in the case of a particular painter. In other cases, however, such as the church, teaching or medicine, there is a well-marked distinction between being a novice, trainee or medical student and becoming a fully fledged practitioner, and the transition from becoming to being a practitioner is marked by the granting of a formal certificate of competence carrying with it an authority to practice. In some societies the transition from childhood to adulthood itself is marked by formal initiation ceremonies. Such clear-cut distinctions are admittedly artificial, but that fact does nothing to undermine the distinction between *becoming* and *being* a person.

6. *Some objections considered*

Finally I would like to consider some objections which might be made to the view that to become educated is to learn to be a person.[12]

(a) It might be pointed out that such an account of education is too abstract to provide teachers and intending teachers with the practical guidance which they need.

It is true that the account is abstract and that it does not provide any direct practical guidance. But this is a consequence of the fact that it is intended as a philosophical account of what different educational practices have in common in being educational rather than, say, medical, economic or religious practices. Its abstraction is therefore a result of its generality, that is, its attempt to say something about all educational practices and their traditions. Comparisons between educational practices, drawing attention to their differences and similarities, may be useful in deepening our understanding of our own educational practice, but that is not what has been attempted here. Moreover, it was argued in Chapter 2 that the view that *a priori* practical principles can be discovered solely through the use of reason is mistaken. In so far as practical principles may be said to exist at all, they exist only as part of the social practices which they guide. If those practices disappear, then the principles embedded in them will disappear also, since they have no independent existence. It is therefore a mistake to expect philosophers or, indeed, educational theorists, to provide such principles. As has been argued earlier, an educational practice is guided primarily by its own educational tradition and the ideal of a person which it provides, although within such a tradition there is room for disagreement and innovation. It is the very existence of the tradition which makes disagreement and innovation possible, just as creativity in painting is made possible by an established painting tradition. The account of the concept of a person which has been offered was intended to be neutral as between the different ideals of a person put forward by different educational traditions and the societies to which they belong. What the latter do indeed is add content and commitment to the abstract logical framework provided by the former; for example, a Christian view of education would be guided by a Christian ideal of what a person ought to be.[13]

(b) The view that to become educated is to learn to be a person cannot be correct, it might be claimed, because persons do not have to learn to be persons; they are persons from the moment they are born.

In replying to this claim, it is first necessary to distinguish the concept of a person from that of a man. Locke's basic definition of a person, it will be recalled, is that a person is an animal that thinks, although in accepting that definition it was stipulated that a person's thought must have a certain degree of complexity. Our idea of a man, on the other hand, 'is nothing else but of an animal of such a certain form'.[14] It follows from these definitions that a cat or a parrot which could think would not be a man, although it would be a person; whereas a man who could not think would still be a man, although not a person. Even if this distinction is accepted its importance could still be overlooked, since it might be claimed that as a matter of fact the only animal which can think is man. But the question whether any animals apart from man can think, although interesting, is not immediately relevant. The point is that the concept of a man (or a human being) is a biological concept, whereas that of a person is not. Although a man becomes a man simply by being born it does not follow that the same is true of a person. Being an animal and, arguably, a man is necessary for being a person but it is not sufficient. Frogs and snails are animals but cannot think, nor can some men, for example Locke's 'children and idiots'. In order to decide how a man becomes a person it is necessary to consult the facts. It could have been the case that babies were born able to think just as well as adults but in fact they are not. They have to acquire what they need in order to become persons after birth, and they do so partly through a process of development and partly by learning. The difference between learning and development was discussed earlier in section III of the previous chapter. Both development and learning are needed in order to become a person, since intelligence – that is, the ability to learn – itself develops with age; but it is the need for learning which provides the scope for education and allows becoming educated to be defined as learning to be a person.

(*c*) An objection which is closely related to the one just considered is that although being educated is a matter of degree, being a person is not. A person can be more or less educated, but not more or less of a person. It follows that the view that to become educated is to learn to be a person cannot be correct.

This objection depends on the view that being a person is *not* a matter of degree, since it is uncontentious that being educated *is*. Two possible sources of that view will be considered – Descartes and Kant. The use of the method of doubt led Descartes to claim that he could not doubt that he was thinking, since any such doubt would be self-refuting, although it was possible for him to doubt the existence of the external world, including that of his own body. He concluded that 'I was a substance whose whole essence or nature consists only in thinking' – that is, in being a mind – and that 'the mind by which I am, is wholly distinct from the body'.[15] Since it is obvious that a person such as Descartes possesses a body, the view of a person which results is that of a mind plus the body to which it is joined. But it is the possession of a mind which is regarded as essential to being a person. Moreover, it follows from the way in which the account was developed that possessing a mind – and therefore being a person – is an all or nothing affair. What is essential to the mind is its ability to think and reflect on its own ability in thinking, and it either possesses that ability or it does not. Men possess minds and therefore are persons; other animals do not (as evidenced by their inability to talk) and therefore are not persons. Since a person is complete as a person from the start in having a mind, there is no scope for becoming more or less of a person or for one person to be more or less of a person than any other.

Locke accepted Descartes' view of a person as a union of body and mind and of thought as the essential characteristic of the mind but differed from him in his account of thought. The mind cannot think until it has acquired ideas through experience; it is dependent on the body for the ideas which are the materials of thought. What is immediately relevant is that the more ideas the mind acquires the greater becomes its capacity for thought. As Locke puts it, 'all those sublime thoughts, which tower above the clouds and reach as high as heaven itself, take their rise and footing here' – that is, in the ideas provided by sense and reflection.[16] There is room in Locke's account for the distinction between a child and an adult and for the idea that a child becomes an adult not simply through a biological process of development but also, and more importantly, through his ever-expanding experience of the world. In other words, children become adults by a process of learning. But Locke's individualism was rejected. It was argued that in order to become persons children must learn not only about the physical world but also about the social world, and that in order to do so they learn not only from the world itself but also from other people. And it is only in doing this that they fully become persons.

Kant is the second obvious source of the view that being a person is not a matter of degree. More than any other philosopher, Kant epitomises the Christian view that persons are, above all, moral beings. They are therefore not only moral agents but also subjects of moral respect – that is, moral subjects. As moral agents, they are required to treat other persons only as ends in themselves and never simply as a means to their own ends. Correspondingly, as moral subjects they are entitled to be treated always as ends in themselves and never simply as a means to the ends of others; their own point of view must therefore always be recognised and respected by others.

The fact that persons become moral agents only in the course of growing up is implicitly recognised in the importance generally attached to moral education. There is therefore no need to consider moral agency as such here, since it supports rather than conflicts with the view that persons have to become persons. All that needs to be recalled from the discussion of responsibility in section I of Chapter 4 is that moral agents must be aware of themselves as agents and therefore must see themselves and others as bound by the moral standards of the community to which they belong. What is true, however, is that persons are regarded as subjects of moral respect from the moment they are born or even, in some views, from the moment of conception simply because of their biological origin. There is therefore no question of their *becoming* moral subjects thereafter, and this is taken to show that becoming a person is simply a matter of being born as a member of the human species. That does not follow. It is true that it is our practice to accord moral and legal rights to infants and children, even though they are not yet responsible moral agents themselves, and so to regard them as persons like ourselves in at least some respects. But this does not show that a person becomes a person, even in the restricted sense of being a moral subject, simply by being born. What happens is that the human infant is born into and is immediately part of a society most of whose members are already moral agents and, therefore, capable of seeing others as having rights and deserving moral respect. The infant is therefore a moral subject because it is seen by others *as* a moral subject, and it is seen in that way because it is our moral practice to see children and infants in that way. It is true that they may be seen differently in other societies. Children and infants thus have rights only because they are seen as having them, even though they are not moral agents and have no conception of themselves or others as the possessors of rights. They depend for their possession of rights on others who differ from them in having a conception of themselves and others as possessors of rights. The idea of children as persons in the sense of being moral subjects therefore only makes sense in relation to the idea of others who are persons in the fuller sense of being moral agents. Logically, there could not be a society all of whose members were persons who were moral subjects only. As parents and teachers know to their cost, children see themselves as possessing rights long before they see others as doing so. Some, indeed, never get beyond that stage, but others must do so if any moral community is to result.

(*d*) Finally, it might be pointed out that while the idea of an uneducated person is not self-contradictory it would be if persons became persons only by becoming educated.

This objection rests on an appeal to ordinary language but, as Austin pointed out, ordinary language does not have the last word on these matters.[17] Attention was drawn in (*b*) above to Locke's distinction between a man and a person, and that distinction cannot easily be rejected even though it is not clear that it corresponds to the way we ordinarily use the words 'man' and 'person'. Given that distinction, the idea of an uneducated *man* is not self-contradictory. It might be pointed out, however, that a new-born baby is an example of an uneducated person, which could not be the case if the idea of such a person were self-contradictory. It has been argued that human infants are only persons in a very weak sense, since they are persons only by courtesy of others and not in virtue of what they are in themselves. It may be that they are granted that courtesy because they are potential persons, that is, possess the ability to *become* persons, but if so that hardly supports the objection being considered. In short, newly born babies are wholly uneducated but, since they are not persons in the full sense intended, they are not examples of uneducated persons. In the case of feral children indeed the infant's potential ability to become a person through education is not realised, so that they become neither educated nor persons.

The objection might also be dealt with more straightforwardly on its own terms. When people say that a person is uneducated they usually mean that he has had little or no formal education and, since a distinction was made between formal and informal education in section I, 2 of this chapter, no contradiction is involved in what they say. The real answer, however, is that ordinary language is unclear and imprecise and nowhere more so than when concerned with education. To reject the view that to become educated is to learn to be a person simply because it does not conform to ordinary language therefore is to refuse to take it seriously as a philosophical account, and to such an attitude there is no answer. Anyone who does take it seriously will look not to ordinary language but to the details of the account given in this and the preceding chapters.

NOTES AND REFERENCES

1 INTRODUCTION

1. Douglas Adams, *The Hitch Hiker's Guide to the Galaxy* (Pan Books, London, 1979), pp. 125, 128.
2. See below, p. 12.
3. R. S. Peters, *Education as Initiation* (Evans, London, 1964) pp. 11, 15, 25, 30. Professor Peters' account of the concept of education was developed further in his *Ethics and Education* (George Alan and Unwin, London, 1966), Part I and 'Education and the Educated Man', in R. F. Dearden, P. H. Hirst and R. S. Peters (eds), *Education and the Development of Reason* (Routledge & Kegan Paul, London, 1972).
4. To allow for e.g. postal teaching, teaching interactions might be better described as person-to-person rather than as face-to-face.

2 PHILOSOPHICAL FOUNDATIONS

1. Sir Ernest Gombrich, *Art and Illusion* (Phaidon Press, Oxford, 1959), p. 3.
2. E. Sapir, 'The Status of Language as a Science', *Language*, 5 (1929), 209.
3. F. Waismann, 'Verifiability', in A. G. N. Flew (ed.), *Logic and Language*, first series (Basil Blackwell, Oxford, 1960), p. 140.
4. *John Locke: An Essay Concerning Human Understanding*, abridged and edited by John W. Yolton (J. M. Dent, London, 1977), II, VIII, 12 (p. 59). All references to Locke's *Essay* give book, chapter and paragraph, followed by page reference in Yolton's abridged edition of the *Essay*.
5. Ibid., II, I, 24 (p. 44).
6. Ibid., III, II, 1, 2 (pp. 207–8).
7. In II, VII Locke argues that only our ideas of primary qualities (basically geometrical properties such as shape and size) resemble the qualities which give rise to them, in contrast to our ideas of secondary qualities (colours, sounds and tastes) which do not. Despite the importance of this distinction to Locke himself, I have assumed that it does not affect the basic picture of the mind as a mirror to nature.
8. L. Wittgenstein, *Philosophical Investigations* (Basil Blackwell, Oxford, 1953), Part II, pp. 194–5.
9. W. G. Chase and H. A. Simon, 'Perception in Chess', *Cognitive Psychology*, 4 (1973), 55–81.
10. Plato, *Republic*, translated by Desmond Lee, second edn (Penguin, Harmondsworth, 1974), Plato, Book I, p. 70.

11. Ibid, Book II, pp. 177ff.

12. John Locke, *Second Treatise of Civil Government*, ed. J. W. Gough (Basil Blackwell, Oxford, 1956).

13. Lock himself believed that 'the state of nature has a law of nature to govern it – . . . which . . . teaches all mankind who will but consult it . . .' etc. (Ibid., Chapter 2, para. 6). This amounts to saying that man, as created by God ('men being all the workmanship of one omnipotent and infinitely wise maker. . .') are already social beings. However, I have taken the view that this is a remnant of an earlier natural law tradition, which is not easy to reconcile with the newer view of man put forward in the *Essay*.

14. Locke, *Essay Concerning Human Understanding*, I, III, 2.

15. J. S. Mill, *Utilitarianism* (J. M. Dent, London, 1910), Ch. 4, pp. 32–3.

16. This is the option Locke himself favours in the *Second Treatise*, cf. note 13 above.

17. M. Oakeshott, 'Political Education', in Peter Laslett (ed.), *Philosophy, Politics and Society* (Basil Blackwell, 1963). Professor Oakeshott's lecture was originally delivered at the London School of Economics in 1951.

18. As with Locke, what is described as the Gombrich point of view is put foward as a reasonable extrapolation of his explicit views as quoted earlier.

19. Mill, *Utilitarianism*, pp. 21–4.

3 THE ORGANISATION OF EDUCATION

1. For a fuller treatment, see John Darling, 'Progressive, Traditional and Radical: a Re-alignment', *Journal of Philosophy of Education*, 12 (1978), 157–66.

2. R. Descartes, *Discourse on Method* (J. M. Dent, London, 1912), Part 1, p. 3.

3. I have previously explored the idea of a profession in Glenn Langford, *Teaching as a Profession* (Manchester University Press, 1978), Ch. 2.

4. Cf. ibid., Ch. 3, section 3.

5. Cf. my discussion of educational problems in ibid., Ch. 1, sections 2 and 3.

6. Cf. my discussion of educational theory in ibid., Ch. 4, section 5.

4 ACCOUNTABILITY

1. Jeremy Bentham, 'Introduction to the Principles of Morals and Legislation', in L. A. Selby-Bigge (ed.), *British Moralists* (Dover, New York 1965), p. 341.

2. Trust seems to have received little philosophical attention, but see D. O. Thomas, 'The Duty to Trust', *Proceedings of the Aristotelian Society* (1978–9).

3. Thomas Hobbes, *Leviathan*, ed. M. Oakeshott (Basil Blackwell, Oxford), pp. 82–3.

5. TEACHERS AS OCCUPYING ROLES

1. Marylin Williams, 'Presenting Oneself in Talk: the Disclosure of Occupation', in R. Harre (ed.), *Life Sentences* (Wiley, Chichester, 1976).

2. R. D. Laing, *Self and Others* (Penguin Books, Harmondsworth, 1971), pp. 81–2.

3. Ibid., pp. 101–2.

4. Stephen Pile, *The Book of Heroic Failures* (Macdonald Futura, London, 1980), p. 20.

5. E. Durkheim, *The Rules of Sociological Method* (Collier Macmillan, West Drayton, 1964), p. 1.

6. J. P. Sartre, *Being and Nothingness* (Methuen, London, 1957), p. 59.

7. Tom Stoppard, *Rosencrantz and Guildenstern are Dead* (Faber and Faber, London, 1967), pp. 11, 16, 28 respectively.

8. For example, in Noam Chomsky, *Language and Mind* (Harcourt Brace and World, New York, 1968), p. 10.

6 TEACHING, LEARNING AND THE SOCIAL BASIS OF KNOWLEDGE

1. Mervyn Peake, *Gormenghast* (Penguin Books, Harmondsworth, 1969), pp. 86–7.

2. Professor Peters' attempt to provide such an account, in R. S. Peters, *Ethics and Education* (George Allen & Unwin, London, 1966), Ch. 5, has attracted much criticism, including Glenn Langford 'Values in Education', in Glenn Langford and D. J. O'Connor (eds), *New Essays in the Philosophy of Education* (Routledge & Kegan Paul, London, 1973).

3. Paul H. Hirst, 'What is teaching?', in *Knowledge and the Curriculum* (Routledge & Kegan Paul, London, 1974), p. 102.

4. Antony Flew, 'Teaching and Testing', in *Sociology, Equality and Education* (Macmillan, London, 1976), p. 79.

5. Glenn Langford, 'The Concept of Education', in Glenn Langford and D. J. O'Connor (eds), *New Essays in the Philosophy of Education* (Routledge & Kegan Paul, London, 1973), section 4.

6. Communication is discussed more fully in Chapter 7, section II, 4.

7. R. Descartes, *Discourse on Method* (J. M. Dent, London, 1912), pp. 5, 5 and 8 respectively.

8. Ibid., pp. 10 and 11 respectively.

9. Mary Shelley, *Frankenstein*, in Peter Fairclouth (ed.), *Three Gothic Novels* (Penguin Books, Harmondsworth, 1968).

10. Karl Popper, *The Logic of Scientific Discovery* (Hutchinson, London, 1959), Preface to the First Edition, 1934, p. 13.

11. Cf. Chapter 2, section I.

7 EDUCATION, PERSONS AND SOCIETY

1. Cf. Glenn Langford, *Teaching as a Profession* (Manchester University Press, 1978), Chapter 4, section IV.

2. Locke, *Essay Concerning Human Understanding*, I, I, 1, p. 1.

3. Agency was also discussed briefly in Chapter 3, section II, section II, 2(c) and Chapter 4, section I.

4. Locke, *Essay Concerning Human Understanding*, II, XXVII, 9, p. 162.

5. Ibid., II, VIII, 12, p. 59.

6. Ibid., I, I, 8, p. 5.

7. Ibid., II, VIII, 2, p. 56.

8. Grice's classic discussion of meaning is relevant here; see H. P. Grice, 'Meaning' in P. F. Strawson (ed.), *Philosophical Logic* (Oxford University Press, 1967). Grice's paper was originally published in *Philosophical Review*, 66 (1957).

9. Grice, 'Meaning', p. 44 makes a similar distinction between 'deliberately and openly letting someone know' and 'getting someone to think', on the one hand, and 'telling' on the other.

10. Cf. Glenn Langford, 'Persons as Necessarily Social', *Journal for the Theory of Social Behaviour*, 8, No. 3 (1978).

11. Edmund Burke, *Reflections on the Revolution in France* (J. M. Dent, London, 1910), p. 93.

12. Some of the objections considered here were made by Adrian Thatcher, 'Education and the Concept of a Person', *Journal of Philosophy of Education*, XIV, No. 1 (1980); cf. also my response, Glenn Langford, 'Reply to Adrian Thatcher', *Journal of Philosophy of Education*, XIV, No. 1 (1980).

13. Adrian Thatcher, 'Learning to Become Persons – A Theological Approach to Educational Aims', *Scottish Journal of Theology*, 36 (1983).

14. Locke, *Essay Concerning Human Understanding*, II, XXVII, 8, p. 160.

15. R. Descartes, *Discourse on Method* (J. M. Dent, London, 1912), Part IV, p. 27.

16. Locke, *Essay Concerning Human Understanding*, II, I, 24, p. 44.

17. J. L. Austin, 'A Plea for Excuses', in *Philosophical Papers* (Oxford University Press, 1961), p. 185.

Bibliography

Adams, Douglas, *The Hitch Hiker's Guide to the Galaxy* (Pan Books, London, 1979)

Austin, J. L., 'A Plea for Excuses', in *Philosophical Papers* (Oxford University Press, 1961)

Ayer, A. J., *Language Truth and Logic* (Victor Gollancz, London, 1936)

Bentham, Jeremy, *Introduction to the Principles of Morals and Legislation* in L. A. Selby-Bigge (ed.), *British Moralists* (Dover, New York, 1965)

Burke, Edmund, *Reflections on the Revolution in France* (J. M. Dent, London, 1910)

Burroughs, Edgar Rice, *Tarzan of the Apes* (Random House, New York, 1983)

Chase, W. G. and Simon, H. A., 'Perception in Chess', *Cognitive Psychology*, 4 (1973), 55–81

Chomsky, Noam, *Language and Mind* (Harcourt Brace and World, New York, 1968)

Darling, John, 'Progressive, Traditional and Radical: a Re-alignment', *Journal of Philosophy of Education*, 12 (1978), 157–66

Descartes, R., *Discourse on Method* (J. M. Dent, London, 1912)

Durkheim, E., *The Rules of Sociological Method* (Collier Macmillan, West Drayton, 1964)

Flew, Antony, 'Teaching and Testing', in *Sociology, Equality and Education* (Macmillan, London, 1976)

Gombrich, Sir Ernest, *Art and Illusion* (Phaidon Press, Oxford, 1959)

Grice, H. P., 'Meaning', in P. F. Strawson (ed.), *Philosophical Logic* (Oxford University Press, 1967)

Hardie, Charles D., *Truth and Fallacy in Educational Theory* (Teachers College, Columbia University, 1962)

Hirst, Paul H., 'What is teaching?', in *Knowledge and the Curriculum* (Routledge & Kegan Paul, London, 1974)

Hobbes, Thomas, *Leviathan*, ed. M. Oakeshott (Basil Blackwell, Oxford, 1951)

Laing, R. D., *Self and Others* (Penguin Books, Harmondsworth, 1971)

Lancaster, Joseph, *Improvements in Education*, ed. and introduced by David Salmon (Cambridge University Press, 1932)

Langford, Glenn, 'Values in Education, in Glenn Langford and D. J. O'Connor (eds), *New Essays in the Philosophy of Education* (Routledge & Kegan Paul, London, 1973)

Langford, Glenn, 'The Concept of Education', in Glenn Langford and D. J. O'Connor (eds), *New Essays in the Philosophy of Education* (Routledge & Kegan Paul, London, 1973)

Langford, Glenn, *Teaching as a Profession* (Manchester University Press, 1978)

Langford, Glenn, 'Persons as Necessarily Social', *Journal for the Theory of Social Behaviour*, 8, No. 3 (1978)

Langford, Glenn, 'Reply to Adrian Thatcher', *Journal of Philosophy of Education*, XIV, No. 1 (1980)

Locke, John, *Second Treatise of Civil Government*, ed. J. W. Gough (Basil Blackwell, Oxford, 1956)

Locke, John, *An Essay Concerning Human Understanding*, abridged and ed by John W. Yolton (J. M. Dent, London, 1977)

Mill, J. S., *Utilitarianism* (J. M. Dent, London, 1910)

Oakeshott, M., 'Political Education', in Peter Laslett (ed.), *Philosophy, Politics and Society* (Basil Blackwell, Oxford, 1963)

O'Connor, D. J., *An Introduction to the Philosophy of Education* (Routledge & Kegan Paul, London, 1957)

Peake, Mervyn, *Gormenghast* (Penguin Books, Harmondsworth, 1969)

Peters, R. S., *Education as Initiation* (Evans Brothers, London, 1964)

Peters, R. S., *Ethics and Education* (George Allen and Unwin, London, 1966)

Peters, R. S., 'Education and the Educated Man', in R. F. Dearden, P. H. Hirst and R. S. Peters (eds), *Education and the Development of Reason* (Routledge & Kegan Paul, London, 1972)

Pile, Stephen, *The Book of Heroic Failures* (Macdonald Futura, London, 1980)

Plato, *Republic*, trans. Desmond Lee, second ed. (Penguin Books, Harmondsworth, 1974)

Popper, Sir Karl, *The Logic of Scientific Discovery* (Hutchinson, London, 1959)

Sapir, E., 'The Status of Language as a Science', *Language*, 5 (1929)

Sartre, J.-P., *Being and Nothingness* (Methuen, London, 1957)

Scheffler, I., *The Language of Education* (Charles C. Thomas, Springfield, III, 1962)

Shelley, Mary, *Frankenstein*, in Peter Fairclouth (ed.), *Three Gothic Novels* (Penguin Books, Harmondsworth, 1968)

Stoppard, Tom, *Rosencrantz and Guildenstern are Dead* (Faber and Faber, London, 1967)

Thatcher, Adrian, 'Education and the Concept of a Person', *Journal of Philosophy of Education*, XIV, No. 1 (1980)

Thatcher, Adrian, 'Learning to Become Persons – A Theological Approach to Educational Aims', *Scottish Journal of Theology*, 36 (1983)

Thomas, D. O., 'The Duty to Trust', *Proceedings of the Aristotelian Society* (1978–79)

Updyke, John, *Couples* (Penguin Books, Harmondsworth, 1968)

Verne, Jules, *Twenty Thousand Leagues under the Sea* (Chatto & Windus, London, 1956)

Waismann, F., 'Verifiability', in A. G. N. Flew (ed.), *Logic and Language*, first series (Basil Blackwell, Oxford, 1960)

Williams, Marylin, 'Presenting Oneself in Talk: the Disclosure of Occupation' in R. Harre (ed.), *Life Sentences* (John Wiley, Chichester, 1976)

Wittgenstein, L., *Philosophical Investigations* (Basil Blackwell, Oxford, 1953)

INDEX

actions 80–4
  as free 82–3, 117
  as involving self-awareness 81
  as performed by agents 80
  constraints on 91
  criticism of 83–4
  explanations of 90
  justification of 90
  unintended consequences of 86, 91
  see also responsibility
accountability 67, 79–102
  of persons 92–3
  of social entities 93–6
accounts:
  as histories 85
  as stories 84–5
  content of 98–9
  financial 84–5, 98
  of a school 98, 99
  parties to 91–2
  personal involvement in 85–7
  purpose of 89, 90, 96, 99
  reactions to 89–91
adults 66
agent-for-another 55
ambiguous figures 14
animals:
  as acting 81
  as learning by imitation 143–4
  as not socially responsible 81, 83, 172
  communication 141–3
  Fred's ferret 170, 144
apprenticeship 74, 157
atomistic view:
  of ideas 12
  of society 12, 23

of teaching 135
autonomy 66
Ayer, Sir A. J. 2

behaviour:
  Gombrich account of 20, 73
  Lockean account of 19, 20, 73
  of animals 170
  see also actions; science of behaviour
behaviourist concept of man 73
beliefs 80, 82
  awareness of 82
  see also concept of a physical object; learning, cognitive
Bell Telephone company 175
Bentham, J. 93, 94
blackbirds 142, 143, 176, 177
Burke, E. 182
Burroughs, E. R. 182
bus service 110

Captain Nemo 152
Casaubon 153
Cavendish, H. 152, 153
Chase and Simon 14
chess, memory of board position 14
children 48, 49, 51, 57, 92, 137, 145, 160, 161, 167, 173, 189, 190, 191
  feral 192
  see also pupils
chimpanzees 143, 145
Chomsky, N. 120
cogito argument 147, 148, 189
communication 120–1, 141–4, 174–81